Post-Pandemic

About the Author

Jonathan McMahon is a Director and Co-Founder of Green Arbour, a strategic advisory consultancy, and a Trustee and Board Member at National Star, a charity which supports young people with special educational needs. He recently stepped down as Joint Chief Operating Officer at St. James's Place Plc., where he was also Chief Risk Officer until 2016. He started his career as Sir Howard Davies's Private Secretary at the Financial Services Authority in the UK, where he had a ringside seat to the financial effects of the 9/11 terrorist attacks. In his early thirties, he was a Director at the Central Bank of Ireland where he played a leading role in the work to rebuild the economy following the global financial crisis. He was educated at St. Andrews University, The College of William & Mary in Virginia, London Business School and IMD in Lausanne.

Post-Pandemic

12 Lessons in Crisis Management

Jonathan McMahon

The Liffey Press

Published by
The Liffey Press Ltd
'Clareville'
307 Clontarf Road
Dublin D03 PO46, Ireland
www.theliffeypress.com

© 2020 Jonathan McMahon

A catalogue record of this book is
available from the British Library.

ISBN 978-1-9160998-7-6

Printed in Scotland by Bell & Bain.

Contents

Acknowledgements   vii

Prologue: A Short History of a Long Crisis   xi

Introduction   1

1. Out of Road   10
    Lesson #1: No one knows what is going to happen.   14

2. Muscle Memory   21
    Lesson #2: Get out of your bubble.   28

3. At the Storm's Edge   34
    *Lesson #3: Imperfect decisions need to be made
    imperfectly.*   40

4. Repairing a Central Bank   50
    *Lesson #4: People who agree with you are not
    always helping.*   57

5. Failing a Way to Success   64
    Lesson #5: Talk about the real issues.   78

6. Eastern Front   84
    *Lesson #6: Don't just understand the numbers,
    understand their meaning.*   97

7. Waiting for Ashoka   108
    Lesson #7: Finding a voice for a crisis.   117

8. Making a Troika   125
    Lesson #8: It is very hard to fix a problem you created. 135

9. The Mother of All Stress Tests   142
    *Lesson #9: Know thyself. The importance of mental
    and physical wellbeing.*   156

10. Taking a Punt   164
    *Lesson #10: Confidence is not competence.
    The uses of doubt.*   173

11. How Much?   179
    Lesson #11: Crises end, but the causes endure.   187

12. Endgame   196
    *Lesson #12: When we fix one crisis we always
    create another.*   207

A Post-Pandemic World   216

Bibliography   249

Index   252

Acknowledgements

First and foremost, this volume is for my parents. They kept a house stocked with books and ideas. So *Post-Pandemic* is by way of thanks to them for these lifelong bequests. It is offered with much love and gratitude.

It is also written in memory of my grandparents. They witnessed most of the crisis-ridden twentieth century, including scenes from its conflicts which were better, if not easily, forgotten. As I wrote this book, I realised how much their stories had influenced and inspired me.

George Beecher, Professor Bruce Gordon and Professor Dale Hoak fostered my interest in history at school and university. I am deeply grateful to them for their inspiration and healthy criticism.

Lyndon Nelson and Adam Shapiro were, in their different ways, brilliant teachers when I entered the world of work. I owe them a lot, not least some of the ideas in this book, as well as their friendship.

I was then fortunate to work for Michael Foot, Sir Howard Davies, Sir Callum McCarthy and Sam Tymms. From them I also learned a lot.

As I wrote this book, I had Michael's voice in my head for much of the journey. The voice of a knowledgeable, wise and kind man. The voice of a man who understands crises, and indeed has created his own fictional one in *Angel Manifesto*.

I owe a special debt of gratitude to Matthew Elderfield for the opportunity to work in Dublin. He was the very model of a leader one would wish to follow in a crisis.

There are many people who hauled Ireland off of the rocks in 2011. I have named only a few of them in the book, but there are many others who deserve credit for their contributions. This includes many former and current employees at the Central Bank of Ireland, the Department of Finance, the National Treasury Management Agency, the International Monetary Fund, the European Commission and the European Central Bank.

Not least among them is Kevin Cardiff. The first draft of history is rarely accurate, nor is it usually fair. In the coming decades, I hope Ireland will come to recognise how fortunate it was to have someone of his integrity and calibre who stood, for so long, on the border between chaos and order.

Myriam Brennan provided the most brilliant support during my time at the Central Bank. An astute observer of human nature, her knowledge of the Central Bank of Ireland helped me navigate those years.

Tara Holness kindly turned my handwritten notes into the first draft of this manuscript (and did much else besides for me at SJP).

I am enormously grateful to them both.

Acknowledgements

The unnamed CEO in the book is David Bellamy, former CEO of St. James's Place Plc. He gave me an opportunity in 2014 to take a new direction, and from him I learned a great deal.

Dwayne Price, Gareth Davis, Phil Gomm and Stuart Cater all read the manuscript. I am grateful to them for their challenging and thoughtful feedback. As I am hugely appreciative of the Reuschs' hospitality in Tennessee as I worked on the manuscript.

Patrick Honohan, Sir Howard Davies, Baroness Patience Wheatcroft, Ashoka Mody, Rory Sutherland and Simon Carswell were also kind enough to read the manuscript and I am hugely grateful for their comments.

I drafted some of this story in my head while crossing the Western Sahara on foot. I am grateful for the companionship of the guys in Tent 69 and, in particular, my friend Jack Price who, without realising it, encouraged me to write the book.

David Givens has been a brilliantly supportive publisher. He's guided me at every turn, not least at the beginning when he gently steered me on a different course. I am honoured to be published by The Liffey Press, as I am grateful for the confidence he has shown in the project.

Jamie Ellul and his brilliant team at Supple Studios designed the cover. They gave me so many great options I was unable to choose and had to outsource the decision to my daughters.

The super creative and talented Freya Wiggin at 145 Studios built my website www.jonathanmcmahon.co.uk. There is more about the book, and a few other things, to be found there.

Katie Read, at Read Media, has provided excellent guidance and support, not least in helping me think through what the book is actually trying to say.

During lockdown, my writing space was commandeered as a home school. A hastily assembled Troika of three daughters quickly asserted its authority, and I was duly assigned a corner of the room. As in Ireland, cohabitation was the right strategy, and it proved the most wonderful way to get to know three wonderful people even better.

Finally, my wife's love and support, given over many years, made this book possible. I can barely begin to express my gratitude.

Prologue: A Short History of a Long Crisis

Ireland has long punched above its weight culturally. This is one of the reasons why there is broad awareness internationally of its financial crisis. But the finer details of the crisis and its resolution are not well known. For this reason, and since the book does not follow a strict chronological order, some explanation of what happened when, and how the chapters fit into an overall timeline, may be helpful.

- In Chapter 1, 'Out of Road', I set the scene for the Irish financial crisis and the dramatic nature of how it unfolded. I then describe my own journey to working at the Central Bank of Ireland in Chapter 2, 'Muscle Memory', and Chapter 3, 'At the Storm's Edge'.

- Chapter 4, 'Repairing a Central Bank', addresses the major problems at Ireland's Central Bank at the time, and the efforts by a fresh team to create a new culture in a moribund institution.

- The Irish State's relationship with its banks is the main focus of Chapter 5, 'Failing a Way to Success'. In an attempt to break the link between the State and the banks, in March 2010 the Irish authorities performed a stress test to see whether the resources existed within the banking system to withstand the crisis. This was followed by an EU-wide stress test with the same objective.

- In Chapter 6, 'Eastern Front', the focus shifts to Anglo-Irish relations. The close economic ties between Ireland and the UK meant that throughout the crisis both countries had a strong interest in each other's destiny. I describe some of the features of this relationship which span the period 2010 to 2012.

- In Chapter 7, 'Waiting for Ashoka', I return to the main story and highlight the wider problems of the Euro Area. These looked to be insoluble until the IMF's dramatic arrival on the scene in November 2010, and in Chapter 8, 'Making a Troika', I describe the days leading up to that pivotal event.

- The IMF's arrival triggered a second attempt to break the toxic link between the Irish State and the banks, again using a stress test. I describe how we approached this task in Chapter 9, 'The Mother of All Stress Tests'.

- Chapter 10, 'Taking a Punt', explores the preparations made to leave the Euro should Plan A, another stress test and more debt, not have worked. It spans the period 2010 to 2012, albeit most of the work was done in 2011 as the Irish authorities pushed hard for fair treatment of the country's debts.

- Finally, the successful, if expensive, conclusion to this story is told in Chapter 11, 'How Much?' and Chapter 12, 'Endgame'.

If this account sounds strangely familiar today, it is because much of the world is staring, post-pandemic, into an economic future as uncertain or worse as that which faced Ireland after 2008. This is why each chapter ends with a discussion of how that chapter's lesson applies to the issues facing us due to the pandemic.

The overall impact is then explored in some detail in the concluding chapter, 'A Post-Pandemic World'.

'By gnawing through a dike, even a rat may drown a nation.'
– Edmund Burke

Introduction

A car crawls its way along a country lane in County Kerry in the southwest of Ireland. The light is fading. The driver is lost. He thinks he recognises some houses in the distance. But he is not certain. A lot has changed in the fifty years since he was last here. There are new roads, and the old ones look unfamiliar. Houses squat in fields which used to lie empty.

He relied on a map to guide him this far. It is the early 2000s, so he does not have a mobile phone or satellite navigation. He is looking for a farm. His uncle's farm. The farm where his mother was born and raised. The farm where he, as a boy, spent the years after the Second World War. Those years when rationing in Britain made it hard to feed four growing boys.

He rounds a bend and stops. There is a herd of cattle in the road. He decides they are not going to move for a while so he gets out to stretch his legs. He looks around. All of a sudden he hears a voice. A voice calling his name.

'Francis. You have been a very naughty boy. Fancy not coming back in all these years.'

Francis is my father and the voice is his cousin's. He has found the farm. And he is staring at its dairy herd, descendant of the one he remembers from his childhood. He pauses and recovers his understanding of the landscape. So much has changed. So much is the same. There is much catching-up to be done over a pot of tea.

We tend to remember those moments when the past breaks forcefully into the present. When we stumble across a memory we have forgotten, or a memory finds us, when we return to a place after a long absence, or when we confront the past in the present.

In his poem, 'The Way Through the Woods', Rudyard Kipling describes how rain reveals a lost track which passes through a woodland. The image reminds us that the past is always with us, even if it is obscured or forgotten. That there are things to be discovered which were, albeit unknown to us, already present. That if, like my father, we stop, get out of the car and look around, we might see or be seen, we might re-find something, we might ourselves be re-discovered.

The two crises which have engulfed the world within one generation, first in 2007, and then in 2020, have worked on the economies and societies as the weather worked to un-cover Kipling's imagined track. In the global financial crisis, we were reminded that banks are inherently fragile, unsta-ble institutions which rely on our confidence in them. And we saw that when they grow too large, they are like daggers poised above the beating heart of an economy. During the COVID-19 pandemic, we saw how massive government in-tervention, as during the Great Depression of the 1930s, is the only thing which can rescue private markets and protect the existing social order. We might have lost our way in the woods before both crises, but politicians and officials quickly found the track which could lead us out to safety.

The American-Canadian author, Donald Kingsbury, made a similar point less obliquely, writing, 'Tradition is a set of solutions for which we have forgotten the problems'. As COVID-19 spread around the globe in 2020, and entire populations suddenly found themselves subject to lockdowns and other restrictions, we adopted patterns of behaviour not seen for generations, at least in the western democracies. Governments also reverted to messages of a type last seen in the 1980s, when we were warned about climbing electricity pylons or mixing cross-ply and radial tyres. Nanny was back. We were urged to wash our hands, limit social contact and ration our purchases of food. We had, in other words, to re-learn traditions which, for our forebears, were habitual.

We call these events crises as they disrupt our lived experience. They also alter our expectations of the future. In these turbulent moments, we feel less sure that the path on which we were travelling goes where we thought. There is a natural instinct for security, the familiar and, perhaps above all else, certainty. No sooner do things change than we want them to return to how we believed they were in the past.

We also want answers. We want to know what went wrong. We turn to our leaders for solutions. Sometimes we look for new people to lead us. There is a clean-up process. We seek signs that the worst is behind us. Politicians, conscious of the electoral cycle, declare victory, usually ahead of time. The cycle repeats.

But what a crisis unmakes is never properly remade. Where an economic or social dislocation cleanses or heals, a system can emerge stronger, fairer, less corrupt and more resilient. A more violent upheaval can often have the opposite effect, leaving damage in its wake. We do not yet know what the events of 2020 mean for the world. But we can say they will have meaning.

The traces of the global financial crisis had not faded by the time COVID-19 spread across the globe in 2020. The 2010s were a decade of sluggish economic performance and, in most major economies, limited growth in public expenditure, if not outright retrenchment and austerity. This left the economic and financial systems of many countries, if not weak, then at least not strong. Historically low interest rates may have helped power stock markets globally to new highs, but such cheap borrowing costs were a sign of weakness, not strength.

Politicians and officials had to work within this damaged legacy to tackle the pandemic. Its effects were almost immediately more far-reaching than those of the financial crisis. Many of us had assumed the earlier crisis was a once-in-a-lifetime experience. In truth, it had not ended when the virus started spreading around the world. As if we were in Kipling's wood ourselves, we saw the tracks of that earlier crisis in both the causes of, and responses to, the economic collapse COVID-19 triggered.

Crises are disruptive. They complicate life. In the middle of the pandemic, we longed for it to end and for the economic damage and social restrictions to be over. But we should not be hasty to return to business as usual. The question we should now be asking is what can be done to escape the effects of the crisis in an enduring way. We should want to build a more resilient social and economic system. We should seek to strengthen the financial system. We should not want to kick these and other problems down the road for future generations to solve.

We did a reasonable job of responding to the global financial crisis, albeit we borrowed our way out of its worst effects. This reflects a habit which has developed in the west to transfer today's responsibilities to tomorrow. A habit memorably satirised in the Simpsons. Shortly before Homer imbibes a noxious combination of vodka and mayonnaise, he explains it will be a problem for 'future Homer', and expresses how he does 'not envy that guy'. He collapses, and we laugh. But we also recognise ourselves.

Will it be different in the 2020s? Democratic societies have responded to crises since 1945 with resolve. This includes the G20's work after the global financial crisis. But even this required strong US backing to make meaningful headway. Today it is hard to see where the impetus will come for a good *apres*-crisis. The technocratic hard yards, which can build resilience into a system, are typically of little interest to politicians. They might subcontract the work to regulators or civil servants. But even when this happens there are often countercyclical forces at work – which lobbyists feed – that frustrate change at precisely the point it is needed. There are many temptations for politicians to leave the bill for delayed renovations to our successors. Like Homer Simpson, we borrow from the future.

The Irish crisis was solved, in part, by doing this very thing: paying back creditors over many years for the failures in economic governance of the 2000s. The global financial crisis came close to bankrupting the Irish State and forcing Ireland out of the euro area. Much work was done to prevent both these outcomes. Some work was done to future-proof the system, but there were many issues left unattended. Why? By 2012, it had proved politically attractive to celebrate the end of the crisis. It was less appealing to do the hard yards in those areas which build resilience in an economy, such as education, banking, housing or transportation. In 2020, Ireland paid the price, and it will continue to do so.

The lessons of the global financial crisis are relevant now as the world measures the consequences of COVID-19. During the worst of the pandemic, politicians and officials showed immense resilience, fortitude and creativity. But they were also making it up as they went along, dealing with imperfect information and, more often than they would ever care to admit, hoping for the best. This was my own experience in Ireland between 2010 and 2012. That was an existential crisis. I suspect it will prove materially less impactful than the pandemic. Its effects will last a generation, if not longer, unless care is taken to make the economy and financial system more resilient.

I started writing this book in Italy in July 2019. My original intention was to produce a guidebook for anyone who might find themselves, as I did, in the midst of a crisis. I had no idea that the towns and villages I visited that summer would soon become the pandemic's European epicentre. There have been many crises during that beautiful land's long history. The Italian peninsula has been ravaged by invasions, conflicts and disease for thousands of years. It has always found a way to recover, to rebuild after an upheaval. It stands as proof that life will continue, if not necessarily as before.

But the rebuilding work does not happen by accident. Life goes on because some people dedicate themselves to the task. My hope is that this book can serve, in its own limited way, as a manifesto for those who believe that the real work of crisis management begins when everyone else has declared victory and gone home. And this reconstruction work is a major undertaking. Not only do we need to recover what we have lost. We have to make ourselves stronger for the next challenge we will, inevitably, come to face.

We will be debating for years whether governments were ready for the pandemic. We will learn some things from retrospective reviews and inquiries, but their inherent theatricality, and politicians' impulse to scapegoat and score points, can obscure the lessons we need to learn. A better use of politicians' time would be to focus on those things which might stop crises from occurring, or at least soften the impact when they do. As Dutch politicians have long known, while there may not be many votes in building sea walls ever higher, there are many lives at stake.

Will we take such a long view? Will we conclude that an economic shock of this magnitude requires better counter-measures? Time will tell. There is a depressingly high likelihood we will apportion blame, score points and find scape-goats. There will be the usual round of institutional reform, which typically amounts to little more than window dressing as brass plates are changed and acronyms revised. Then the circus will move on.

When it does, a few determined souls will work quietly to rebuild and prevent a recurrence. This can be a noble yet lonely occupation. If you are one of these doughty souls, and if this book does nothing else, I hope it keeps you company as you work to address the aftermath of one crisis and get ready for the next.

This book contains some theory, but it is not a theoretical volume. In one way or another, I have been studying crises, or trying to prevent or address their consequences, for twenty years. I have been in the thick of crises in my own career, and I have met plenty of others who have had similar experiences. This book is therefore a personal account of a crisis and crises. An account of those years when Ireland stood on the brink after one of the biggest economic collapse in history.

It is also an attempt to understand how we might climb out of the COVID-19-shaped hole into which the world fell in 2020. In dealing with the virus, governments had no choice but to take exceptional steps to protect public health and the economy. These were merited. But we will live with the consequences of the initial shock, and the policy response, for years to come. It is uncomfortable, but necessary, to recognise that the COVID-19 crisis will not end with a vaccination or mass immunity. The second- and third-round effects will throw up challenges we are yet to observe, let alone comprehend. We need to be ready for them, as we need to think hard about what *might* be around the corner.

If we learn the lessons of the pandemic, and if we can re-learn the lessons of the global financial crisis, we might emerge stronger and more resilient. The earlier crisis had global effects, and although not every nation's banks were implicated, there was an international response. The pandemic merits an even greater effort to strengthen public health and economic systems globally, not least because of the damage it has done to those least able to afford its effects. History shows that when nations abandon cooperation, crises are not only harder to manage, they are more likely to occur in the first place.

History also tells us three things about crises. That they never end when we think (or like to believe). That the causes are ever present, if unseen or overlooked. And, in solving one crisis, we always do things which make the next one more likely. This means that if we are serious about the activity of crisis prevention and management, we must accept the Sisyphean nature of the task. The business of making highly complex and fragile systems safer never ends. Like Sisyphus, we have no choice but to keep pushing.

Unlike Sisyphus, we do have a choice about whether we allow the rock to roll away from us. It is sometimes forgotten that it was the Greek King's misrule, his arrogance and deceitfulness, which led to his punishment in the underworld. Had he been a better ruler, he would not have spent an eternity repeating the same task, making no progress. It is a powerful, highly symbolic story. A metaphor to describe what happens when we do not attend to our responsibilities properly.

This book explains how we can do a better job this time. How we might keep pushing uphill with a purpose, not merely repeat the same, familiar task when we allow the rock to roll away. It identifies the areas where governments and officials ought to focus. And, just in case we do not get it right, and an insurance policy is needed, it is also a guide for the next generation when it faces the consequences of our action and, of course, our inaction.

1.

Out of Road

Once he said that he was from Sinn Féin I didn't register much else. This included his name. It felt like a scene from a film, the scene before the one in which I disappeared. My mind was racing.

I spoke to some colleagues. They laughed.

After a phone call to a friend I felt confident I had identified the caller. Caoimhghín Ó Caoláin, Teachta Dála (TD), or member of the Irish parliament, for the Cavan-Monaghan constituency in Ulster.

My heart rate back under control, I tried to remember what he had said. There was something almost old-fashioned in his manner. He was polite and softly spoken. But what did he want? I looked over the notes I had scribbled as he talked.

He said he wanted to discuss Quinn Insurance. He did not wish to cut across the Central Bank's independence, he added. But he did want to discuss the insurance company which one of the wealthiest men in Ireland, Sean Quinn, owned. He also wanted the Central Bank to understand the consequences of its decision. Putting the insurance company into administration would mean job losses. The context was important. The broader context. Actually, to be precise, the border context. The border between the Republic and Northern Ireland, he emphasised, in case I had not grasped his point. He said he thought we should meet. That weekend, in fact. But not just him. About twenty other politicians from border constituencies.

I doubt I would have remembered the call in such detail had it come from a politician representing a different party. But it didn't. It came from Sinn Féin. To anyone with a memory of the Troubles in Northern Ireland, Sinn Féin was never a neutral political brand. In the six counties, it meant one thing to one group of people and the opposite to another. That I momentarily lost myself during the call did not surprise me then. Nor does it surprise me today, over a decade later.

But the name was not just an echo from the television and newspaper reports of my childhood. It was an echo from my own family's history. My Irish grandmother had talked about Sinn Féin around the dining room table at family gatherings. Except this was the Sinn Féin of the 1920s. In her final months, when she was dying of cancer, she told me about how she had witnessed the Irish Civil War first-hand. How it marked her childhood in Kerry. These conversations were not only my introduction to Sinn Féin. They proved how hard it can be to grow up in an Irish family and not discuss history, especially in an émigré family. So when Caoimhghín Ó Caoláin called me late in the day in early April 2010, the moment was rich with significance. Ireland's past was excavating itself, once more, in the present.

Not that there was time to dwell on these thoughts. The reason why twenty border politicians wanted to travel to Dublin only became clear over the coming months. The

Central Bank's decision to put Quinn Insurance into administration triggered a chain of events without precedent in Irish corporate history. The business empire Sean Quinn had built, over many decades, began to unravel in a matter of months. What had been a successful conglomerate fast became a tangled mess of failed businesses.

We did not know this when we met Caoimhghín Ó Caoláin and his colleagues. We did not know how many jobs were at risk. We had little idea about the depth of the problems in the group. All we knew for sure was that Quinn Insurance had run out of road. We also knew it was a test for the Central Bank. A test of a regulator which, for years, had been regarded as weak. A test of a regulator which, in the opinion of many, had failed to prevent a crisis. A test of a regulator with a new leadership team. A test of a regulator which had emphasised its own independence. A regulator committed to enforcing the law. Free from political influence. Beyond the reach of financial sector lobbyists. The stakes were therefore high.

The politicians knew these things. The banking crisis reached deep into the day-to-day life of their constituents. They had seen the criticisms of the regulator, seen the change of guard at Dame Street, its headquarters. They understood why the government had made a big thing of regulatory independence. But they needed to test whether the Central Bank was completely serious about its independence. Whether it was serious about keeping Quinn Insurance in administration.

At first they went through the motions. They all said they respected the Central Bank's independence. But they wanted the Central Bank to understand the risks of sticking to its decision.

'What would happen if Quinn Insurance could not trade?' they asked. 'Why can't it be allowed to trade?'

They were not wrong to ask these questions as jobs were at risk. But inferring there to be a trade-off between the regulator's independence and livelihoods in Cavan, the small border town home to the Quinn Group, was an error of judgement. This had been one of the cardinal mistakes of the 2000s. It was one of the reasons why Quinn Insurance and most of the banking system was close to collapse.

They left without the answer they wanted. Or did they? I suspect they had some hope, before the meeting, that the Central Bank might make an exception for Quinn Insurance. That it would ease its requirements and allow it to restart trading. Otherwise why bother travelling to Dublin? But during the meeting I could see opinions shift. No one who listened to the experienced, senior official, Patrick Brady, could have doubted that the problems were real and serious. They could not have doubted that Quinn and his team had brought most of these problems on themselves. Nor could anyone have doubted these problems left the Central Bank with very few options, especially if independence was to mean anything. As the meeting wore on, and the facts of the situation were laid bare, I sensed the politicians accepted our version of events. Certainly no one disputed that the Central Bank needed to be able to do its job.

Perhaps a different conversation might have taken place in the mid-2000s. Perhaps it would have occurred in Cavan. Perhaps with Sean Quinn himself in the room. Perhaps the Central Bank would have stood down. A solution would have been found to keep corporate Ireland motoring. Job done. But none of this happened. Thanks to the law of unintended consequences, a different story was written that day. A story which allowed Ireland to change, and for the better. Strange as it may seem, Sean Quinn saved Ireland.

Lesson #1: No one knows what is going to happen.

In ancient Rome, some citizens, known as haruspex, were trained to inspect the entrails of sacrificed animals in order, so it was believed, to read the future. They were particularly fond of the livers of poultry and sheep. One haruspex, Spurinna, on reportedly finding a bull without a heart, is said to have warned Julius Caesar that his time might be up if he stayed in Rome. A few days later, the Roman dictator was assassinated, although we have no idea if he heeded the prophecy or not.

It is human to want to understand the future. It is human to dislike uncertainty, or at least to prefer certainty. And some humans, like haruspex, seek to sound authoritative and confident about the future. I have yet to meet anyone who can see the future. But if we have learned anything in the past two decades, it is that political and economic predictions have more in common with chicken entrails than today's soothsayers might care to admit.

Crises change how we think about the future. Our settled assumptions are altered, sometimes radically, usually unexpectedly. We might want to believe that there is order in the world, and that historical change is gradual. But for most of human time, sudden, unanticipated and sometimes violent events have shaped our experience. Ultimately, we find ways to cope with these events. But there is always a process of adjustment. Whether at the level of an individual, an organisation or an entire society, disruption of our settled assumptions can be disturbing. Is it any wonder we are attracted to those who make some claim to foresight?

❄   ❄   ❄

The COVID-19 pandemic is a case study in uncertainty. That no one knew how the virus would spread was, very early on, abundantly clear. It was equally clear that there was not a settled idea about how to stop its spread, with different countries following different approaches. This uncertainty put pressure on our leaders. Those who acknowledged the uncertainty looked and sounded more plausible and realistic. Those who claimed to understand the virus, or who were sanguine about the outbreak, looked increasingly ridiculous as the outbreak escalated.

These different reactions tell us much about how humans process uncertainty. Those leaders who struggled to comprehend the situation, whether because they underestimated events or were simply out of their depth, proved slower to develop credible responses. Those leaders who accepted the inherent uncertainty, and did not pretend to know what might happen, had already made the emotional and intellectual leap required to solve the problem. We know from our own lives that we sometimes under-prepare for situations or encounters. The pandemic reminded us of the consequences when an entire country exhibits this tendency. In a crisis, it is dangerous to pretend things might be more certain than they are in reality.

The leader's task is to confront reality, to understand the nature of the uncertainty, not to avoid it or wish it away. It is also their responsibility to galvanise a response. In a crisis, however, leaders, and the people around them, will themselves experience powerful emotions. These can lead to fear, anxiety or reticence, all of which can be disabling. It can also trigger the opposite response with overconfidence, in its various forms, leading to bold or hasty actions, or sometimes no action at all. All of these reactions impair the search for solutions.

But a crisis also creates an opportunity for a determined leader. In a situation of uncertainty, people look for direction. We saw this during the COVID-19 pandemic. Those leaders who found a way to talk about the issues honestly, while also providing a sense of resolve, were the most convincing, and rightly earned praise for their handling of events. By common consent, Angela Merkel, the German Chancellor, and Jacinda Ardern, the Prime Minister of New Zealand, found this balance. They were almost certainly helped by effectual government action. But there can be little doubt that they, in turn, enabled effectual government.

The excessively confident leader, by contrast, can make a crisis worse. Risks are discounted. The likely effects are downplayed. We have seen this reaction in both recent crises. The bank executives who underestimated the problems they were facing as the global financial crisis took hold. Those who, in the early stages of the COVID-19 outbreak, misread the risks or were slow to prioritise public health measures.

Those naturally bullish personalities, such as Donald Trump or Boris Johnson, who appeared to take just a little too long to correct their initial, overly sanguine reactions.

This should not be surprising. The overly confident individual is less likely to worry about the future. They are more likely to want to make bold decisions, to do something, to be seen to act and to want to appear strong. But grand gestures have lasting consequences. And people die when we discount hazards and do not allow for harmful eventualities. Confidence is not the same as competence (see Lesson #10).

A different sort of confidence is required in a crisis. The confidence to wait and see how a situation develops. The sort of confidence to listen and observe, rather than speak and act. The individual likely to make better decisions in a crisis is the one who seeks to understand first and decide second. This is certainly one of the lessons of the global pandemic. And it is a lesson which looked like it may have been forgotten in the age of populist politicians.

One of the ironies of the outbreak is that it occurred after many years during which populist politicians had confidently advocated simple solutions to complex problems. COVID-19 was anything but a simple problem. Very quickly we saw the benefits of having thoughtful leaders listening to experts. The benefits, as it were, of political pragmatists, officials and experts working in tandem. We saw what is possible when evidence, rather than opinion or prejudice, informs decisions.

More obliquely, both the global financial crisis and the pandemic have demonstrated the difficulties of dealing with that wellspring of uncertainty: complexity. As we learned in 2008, there is nothing simple about the financial system. Similarly, the all-consuming effects of the virus have shown just how intricately woven the fabric of the modern economy has become. Governments have been pushed to the edge of their capabilities to deal with the dual consequences of uncertainty and complexity. During the COVID-19 outbreak, we saw world leader's grappling with fragmentary and sometimes conflicting evidence as they sought to control, and then manage, the impact of the virus. As during the global financial crisis, it was painfully obvious that neither our elected representatives, nor their chosen advisers, knew what was going to happen.

But it is possible to simplify complex systems. As it is possible to train leaders to manage uncertainty and complexity. Thanks to the work of academics who have studied human decision making, we have a better understanding of how we think. The celebrated behavioural economists, Daniel Kahneman and Amos Tversky, demonstrated in their 1974 paper, 'Judgement Under Uncertainty', how our brains try to cope with uncertainty. They showed how we respond to complexity. How we can, in the course of assessing incomplete or contradictory information, impair our own judgement. This research does not mean we are destined to make a mess of high-pressure, uncertain situations. But it does show we will find them inherently challenging. With training, however, we can at least be aware of our limitations, as we can work to overcome them. As the Canadian test pilot and astronaut, Chris Hadfield, put it, 'anticipating problems and figuring out how to solve them is actually the opposite of worrying: it's productive'.

Leaders in all fields will have to anticipate problems, devise solutions and address complex systems in the years to come if we are to build greater resilience into public health and economic systems. We are already aware of some of the pandemic's legacy. But we do not understand the totality of its effects. It is unlikely we will do so for at least a decade. Nor can we say, nor should we conclude, we have seen the worst of a pandemic in COVID-19. We also cannot say how the indirect public health consequences, physical and mental, might manifest themselves in the years to come.

This is not to comment on the nature or frequency of mass outbreaks of communicable diseases. It is simply to recognise that we do not understand the future. The leaders who accept this truth, and who embrace the inherent uncertainty of the situation, will be those who trigger a search for better answers. They will be those who explore different scenarios, who act to make the world a more resilient and safer place. Those fearful of the future or, conversely, excessively sanguine, are likely to fail in this basic duty to current and future generations.

Some lessons for leaders in a crisis:

1. **To reduce uncertainty, reduce complexity.** Leaders have no choice but to operate in uncertain environments. You cannot alter these conditions, but you can address one source of uncertainty: complexity. Many organisations develop structures and processes which are not only unnecessarily complex, but which make it harder to manage an operation and understand its risks. A crisis will expose all of the resulting complications, possibly too late.

2. **Prepare**. The quality of your response to a crisis will, to a large degree, depend on how well you have prepared yourself. You can improve your own self-knowledge. You

can also read the stories of those who have operated in conditions of uncertainty. A responsible leader is prepared and historically informed.

3. **Always be looking for the next problem.** It is a leader's responsibility to address the known consequences of uncertainty. It is also their responsibility to explore scenarios which might reveal unknown consequences. This boils down to asking better questions about how the future might diverge from the present.

2.

Muscle Memory

The views from the seventh floor of the Central Bank of Ireland's former headquarters on Dame Street were impressive. There were cranes everywhere on the Dublin skyline. Traffic was backed-up along the river. The Celtic Tiger was in full swing. But Patrick Neary, the Financial Regulator's CEO, looked concerned when Con Horan, the Head of Supervision, entered his office. Neary excused himself and left the room. I could tell he was wearing a brave face when he returned a few moments later.

It was 2007 and I was in Dublin to complete a project for the Financial Regulator on its oversight of the Irish Stock Exchange. I had no idea then that I would come to spend hundreds of hours in that same office two years later. I had no idea what would happen to the Irish banks. Patrick Neary had no idea that he would be eviscerated on Irish television. All of these things lay ahead.

But in his whispered conversation with Con Horan, I can now see the first stirrings of that crisis which was soon to overtake Ireland. I have never asked Con why he interrupted Patrick Neary that day. I think it is unlikely he would remember. There were so many problems surfacing in 2007 that it

21

NF/242

could have been one of many. But their mutual look of concern told its own story. It was a look I was to see again and again on the faces of Irish officials in the coming years. Only in 2012, five years later, did fear start to give way to hope.

I was fortunate to witness the beginning and the end of the Irish financial crisis. That I was there at all was a complete accident. I had been earning a decent living as a consultant. The work was interesting, I was seeing the world, and I liked my colleagues. I had no desire to change this comfortable arrangement.

That is until Matthew Elderfield, the recently appointed CEO of the Irish Financial Regulator, called me in November 2010. I made the decision immediately but spent the following weeks trying to talk myself out of it. I had a nice life, and we lived in a nice part of the world. Our eldest daughter was in a good school, which had settled that perennial preoccupation of new parents. All of this I weighed carefully. Perhaps overcompensating for my impulsive first response, I spent hours debating my choices, walking my dog into the ground in the process. I knew what I wanted, but what would I give up?

I believed I was ready for the challenge. Early in my career, I had served as the Private Secretary to Michael Foot, Sir Howard Davies and Sir Callum McCarthy, Managing Director and the first two Chairmen of the Financial Services Authority (FSA). These were three of the most experienced and capable public servants then working in Britain. It was a brilliant education, during which I witnessed how complex and difficult decisions are made. How choices are weighed, and how competing objectives are evaluated. How leaders operate under pressure, and how they cope with inadequate information.

And it was a period of mini-crises. The collapse of Equitable Life. The failure of split-capital investment trusts. The implosion of the hedge fund, Long Term Capital Management. The emergency nationalisation of Railtrack (now National Rail). The collapse of Independent Insurance. I saw all of this first hand. I was not a decision-maker, but I could not have been closer to the action. It was intoxicating, and when it stopped nothing felt like it could ever be as good again. Until Ireland, that is.

Of these events, the one which had the most impact on me was the terrorist attack of 11 September 2001. On the day when the planes struck New York and Washington D.C., I was working in the shadow of Canary Wharf Tower, one of the tallest buildings in London. My desk was only a few feet away from where the FSA's leadership team sat. That day, however, none of them were in the office. In fact, my boss at the time, Managing Director, and effective number two to Howard Davies, Michael Foot, was in Paris. That left me and my opposite number, Adam Shapiro, to hold the fort. So as stock markets plunged, and the phones started to ring, we did what we had seen done to manage other issues. We pulled the key people into one room to get the best possible read on the situation and to coordinate follow-up activity.

In the immediate aftermath of the attacks, no one knew what was going on, but everyone could see the political and market reaction. Our first concern was for the physical safety of people in the building. Canary Wharf was an obvious target. It had been bombed by the IRA in the 1990s. As the FCA was also responsible for the orderly functioning of stock markets, we had to work out what to do about an increasingly disorderly market. There was also a risk that individual financial institutions might come under pressure, especially those, like Cantor Fitzgerald, who were directly affected. But we also had to be mindful of indirect effects. Financial markets are susceptible to rumours; hearsay can make even the strongest institutions vulnerable.

During the following days, we established a crisis management centre to coordinate all of the work and to communicate with the outside world. This involved regular contact with officials in the United States and the UK, including the security services. I was too busy making sure Howard and Michael had everything they needed to take it all in at the time. But I do recall being impressed by their ability to remain calm enough to ask the right questions at the right time. It was an immersive experience, in the course of which I started to build some of the crisis management muscle memory which would help me later in Dublin.

Matthew Elderfield was in the crisis room in those weeks. He was responsible for oversight of stock markets at the FSA. Although we knew one another, I had not worked with him closely until that point. After I left the FSA in 2006, I saw him next in Bermuda in 2008, where he was Chief Executive of the Bermuda Monetary Authority. He invited me to dinner at his house outside the capital city, Hamilton. We swapped stories about what our former colleagues were doing. Matthew talked about his path to Bermuda, and explained the island's history and politics. It was an enjoyable, relaxing evening, if surreal given the backdrop of a global financial crisis gathering momentum.

I was in Bermuda because of this crisis. I was working for Promontory Financial Group. It had grown quickly on the back of assignments for financial institutions which had run into trouble. Promontory's founder, the charismatic Eugene Ludwig, started the firm after completing an assignment for Allied Irish Banks. It had appointed him to investigate trading losses at its US subsidiary, Allfirst. Promontory quickly became the specialist in dealing with those blow-ups which occur frequently in financial services. As the global financial crisis built a head of steam, Promontory was ideally positioned to repeat similar exercises. This was not quite a licence to print money, but it did leave the firm with fantastic prospects.

By then I was becoming an expert in failing banks and crises. I could not have chosen a more marketable career. In 2007, I cut my teeth at Royal Bank of Scotland, soon to be the poster child for everything wrong about banks and banking. Promontory had been engaged to do a fairly mundane piece of work for its risk team. This meant regular travel to Gogarburn, its headquarters outside Edinburgh. This new complex, which RBS described as a campus and which contained its own supermarket, could have been designed for a bond villain.

When I arrived at Gogarburn, the storm clouds were gathering over the bank. Not that anyone seemed to have noticed. RBS retained the swagger and confidence for which it became notorious. It was, truth be told, full of itself. It was also sinister. There were constant hushed, reverential references to Sir Fred Goodwin, RBS's CEO. He was everywhere, even when he was somewhere else. It was disconcerting to watch well-educated, successful people running around saying,

'Fred said this' or 'Fred said that'. The cult of personality was all pervasive. Apparently he even chose the fabric for the office chairs.

At RBS sensible people allowed themselves to believe things that were not true about their own bank. At Bermuda's second largest bank, Butterfield, where I was sent in 2008, sensible people allowed themselves to believe things that were not true about someone else's bank. Although its errors were much smaller than those made at RBS, they threatened to be no less fatal. Butterfield's management had swallowed a sales pitch from Wall Street bankers eager to offload mortgage-backed securities. When the underlying borrowers stopped paying their mortgages, the value of the security Butterfield had purchased dropped. When the true toxicity of its new investment became apparent, the bank found itself staring at a large loss. Promontory was called in to understand what had gone wrong. We also had a brief to help the bank climb out of the hole it had dug for itself.

My work at RBS and Butterfield taught me some invaluable lessons. At RBS, I saw first-hand the effects of a culture gone wrong. At Butterfield, I started to understand what could happen when risk was not properly evaluated. Not that I appreciated the importance of this education at the time. Nor did I have any idea that I would soon cease to be a spectator to the spreading financial crisis. But in the summer of 2008, like everyone else, I was left speechless as some of the great names in finance toppled: Northern Rock, Bear Stearns, AIG, Lehman. The list grew longer each month. Those not absorbed by competitors fell into government ownership. Something was evidently badly wrong with the financial system. This was alarming in its own right. But what made it really worrying was what makes all crises worrying: uncertainty. No one knew where it would end or how bad things might become.

The crisis peaked when I was least able to follow what was happening. In the summer of 2008, I was in the English Lake District. The remote hills and fells of Cumbria were a long way from the trading floors in London and New York where the drama was unfolding. This contrast was not lost on me. But my livelihood depended on knowing what was going on in financial markets. I had clients in the eye of the storm. My colleagues were in the thick of things. But where was I? At the end of a long length of copper in the middle of nowhere, battling a dial-up modem for information. If the crisis was painful, trying to follow it using 1990s infrastructure, in somewhere which felt like it was still in the 1890s, was excruciating.

After a while, I gave up. It was simply too frustrating. I opened my wallet, checked I had some cash, pulled on my shoes and walked to the local pub. No one at the bar seemed too concerned. The world may have been teetering on the edge of a second Great Depression, or worse, but the pints of beer were still flowing in the Boot Inn.

Perhaps my sense of complete powerlessness, the feeling of being no more than a helpless spectator, made me more susceptible to Matthew's invitation in November 2009. By then Butterfield had found a way to limp on, RBS was in government ownership, and the global economy was in a state of shock. Matthew had also moved. He had made his own journey from Bermuda to Ireland to become CEO of the Financial Regulator, the post Patrick Neary had vacated.

Matthew knew he would have many problems on his hands in Dublin. But he could not have known how many.

Nor could anyone else. Matthew's boss, the new Governor, Patrick Honohan, had only recently been appointed himself. He was an acknowledged expert in financial crises. He knew that Ireland's situation was perilous. But I suspect not even Patrick understood exactly how difficult things were going to become. The coming years would test everything he had learned.

And despite having spent years studying crises, he had never actually had to manage one. In fact, none of us had managed a banking crisis. None of us had managed a sovereign debt crisis. None of us had tried to keep a country within a currency union which many feared might disintegrate. Still, we were confident. But would this be enough?

Eventually I made my decision in response to Matthew's invitation. A new chapter was about to begin.

Lesson #2: Get out of your bubble.

The best and least well-informed profession is that of the taxi driver. This is true everywhere in the world, and it was true before globalisation.

In Dublin I was a regular user of taxis, typically to and from the airport. The drivers were either in extreme debt (typically the younger ones) or had no debt at all (typically the older ones). It was hard to find one with manageable or moderate personal debt. The really unlucky ones had bought a new taxi just before the crisis struck. And this group of unfortunates included those who had purchased a luxury German marque.

I always listened to taxi drivers, and not in the sense that everyone *has* to listen to taxi drivers. I listened because they know what is going on, even if they don't always know why. In London in 2006, a cabbie once asked me how he might get a mortgage for a Romanian property. My existing suspicions about a frothy market further aroused, I sold my flat in London that summer, not long before property prices crashed.

In Dublin I listened because I could find out what was really going as I sat in the back seat, passing through the Port Tunnel or North Dublin. The enforced autobiography of a taxi journey is, in its own way, the biography of a city or nation. No one driver could describe everything which had led Ireland to this point in its history. Nor was there a driver waiting at Dublin airport who could explain everything which was happening as the Celtic Tiger unwound its grip on the country. But as I gathered the drivers' stories, I was able to interpret what was going on in the country. I sometimes wish I had recorded the conversations for a work of social anthropology. It could have become a classic work: 'What the feck's actually happening here?'

The anthropologist, Clifford Geertz, talked about the importance of 'thick description'. By this he meant that we should always work harder to find out the meaning of the things we observe, and to avoid superficial judgements. As time went on, I became better at asking the questions which elicited a 'thicker' description. This amateur sleuthing revealed that most of these men (and they were almost all men) knew Ireland had faced tougher times. This was a largely unconscious belief, but no less powerful for being so. Underneath all of the superficial grumbles was usually this concession: 'Sure, my mother and father had it more difficult.' This suggested to me that Ireland would work its way out of the crisis. It did not indicate that the Irish would accept unlimited pain, but it did confirm a measure of resilience among the population.

❄   ❄   ❄

It was not, of course, possible to take taxis, or at least not easily, during the COVID-19 pandemic. It was, though, easy enough to discover what people were thinking through social media channels. Unlike the national broadcast media, which tends to report in a top-down way, social media channels give a bottom-up perspective on what is actually happening in day-to-day lives. This was particularly useful during the lockdown. It was possible to track the shifting mood as we moved through the different phases of the pandemic, from the selfless reaction at the start, to the growing anxiety about jobs and income. I deliberately followed people outside my own network, in areas of life of little interest to me in normal times, to try to gauge the mood among the public. This was my taxi ride during the pandemic.

This is, by its very nature, imperfect research. It is unlikely to provide any crisis-altering revelations. But this is not the point. The alternative is to remain within a bubble, and this will reveal nothing you do not already know. It is easy to surround yourself with likeminded people. Easy to defer to the data. Easy to believe that what the media is reporting is what a country is thinking. The challenge in a crisis is to find out what is really going on, especially in a situation where there is heightened uncertainty and doubt.

So much of what happens at the top of government, and in large organisations, occurs within an echo chamber. This is not a criticism of the highly able people who fill the top jobs. But they tend to look similar, sound similar, think the same things and act in similar ways. This is because they are similar. And I should know as I was one of these people. I have lived inside the echo chamber.

It is easy to believe that the people who happen to be in charge when a problem surfaces are the right people to solve that problem. But in a crisis, diversity of thought is needed. Otherwise the frame of reference is too narrow and consensus wins out. Technocrats, unsurprisingly, like technocratic solutions. But technocratic solutions are not the only answers, nor always the right ones. Having someone in the room willing to ask 'will it work?' is invaluable.

As governments and parliaments start to assess how the COVID-19 pandemic was handled, there will be a lot of discussion about how decisions were made. A key area of focus will be how politicians and officials found out what was happening during the early stages of the outbreak. Do not be surprised if the response comes in graphs and charts, the minutes of meetings, official reports. These are entirely legitimate and valuable sources, but they are not the only sources. We need to understand how our leaders enriched their understanding of the issues. How they found out what people were thinking and doing. How they calibrated policies to take account of what was happening on the ground, and what factors might therefore influence or alter these policies unintentionally.

I was fortunate to work for a chief executive who understood the need to obtain information from a range of sources, not just the information presented to him. He had a large common sense filter. He knew that data is unreliable as it contains mistakes and omissions. He also knew that it is rarely neutral. Data is presented for a reason. He thought it was his job, as the man in charge, to understand these reasons.

He also knew it would be foolhardy to run the company from a distant eyrie, being fed a diet of numbers by accountants and actuaries. He was able to move between flying the company on its financial dials and piloting it using intuition, experience and his understanding of what was happening at the coalface. This enabled him to puncture that bubble which so easily forms around senior leaders.

It helped that he had worked his way up through the company. He had performed many different functions, which is unusual for most contemporary leaders, especially in politics. Politicians have little, if any, experience of running organisations, of making things work. Combined with a bubble existence, this lack of practical experience is problematic in the normal course of events. In extreme situations, political leaders can find themselves divorced from reality and faced with responsibilities beyond their competence. In a crisis, dealing with reality and making things work is the name of the game.

The coming decades will require high levels of competence and problem-solving abilities in our political leaders. In a complex and uncertain world, it is harder than ever to ascertain the reality of a situation. In their critique of mainstream politicians, populists tend to gloss over the complexity of the modern world. But they did get one thing right: some of those in charge had become detached from reality. Being inside a bubble had become a problem, and voters sensed it. The next decade is going to be incredibly challenging, and our leaders would do well not to retreat to the echo chamber when things become difficult. If they do, they will be inviting the sort of political backlash which will lead to a crisis of a very different, and possibly very dangerous, kind.

Some lessons for leaders in a crisis:

1. **Find out for yourself what is happening.** What a leader is told is happening is not always the same as what is *actually* happening. A leader needs to close this gap by finding reference points outside the bubble.

2. **Diversity of thought matters.** It is easy for a leader to surround themselves with people who are similar. If this is the case, the outer edges of the bubble will be even thicker than normal, and getting a grip on reality that much harder. Diversity of thought will not necessarily burst the bubble, but it will make it more permeable.

3. **Know when you are in the bubble.** People at the top can sometimes believe they have all the answers available to them, if only they ask the right questions. This is classic bubble thinking, and it leads to closed-loop decision-making processes. A leader needs to understand when the process they are using to make decisions is excessively insular.

3.

At the Storm's Edge

On the morning of my interview at the Central Bank, I was running late for my appointment, I was nervous, and I was walking the wrong way along Grafton Street, Dublin's main shopping thoroughfare.

Although the hotel where I was staying was just along the River Liffey from the Central Bank, I had managed to get lost. Being a man, I resisted asking for directions. But the clock was running down. There was a life-changing interview ahead of me. This was not the day to explore the city. I looked at my watch. I was due to be with Matthew Elderfield and Patrick Honohan in ten minutes. I decided to swallow my pride and ask for directions. But it was a wet day in November 2009, during a deep recession, and Grafton Street was empty. The only person I could see was a large leprechaun holding a sign advertising a Footwear Sale.

My Irish grandmother specialised in giving her family strange gifts at Christmas. One of her more bizarre offerings was a leprechaun. I remember holding the wrapped box thinking it must be an Action Man. My disappointment was therefore multiplied when, rather than seeing Eagle Eye rigged in full camouflage staring back at me, instead I found myself looking upon a soft toy with a sinister grin and a giant mop of ginger hair.

All of this came back to me in slow motion as I looked towards the much larger relative of my own unwanted bequest on Grafton Street. Was I really going to have to ask a leprechaun how to get to the Central Bank? He looked friendly enough, so I walked towards him and struck up a conversation. I think he was glad to be asked. It was a cold day. There was little interest in his Footwear Sale. Speaking through his nylon beard, he tactfully pointed out that I was walking in the wrong direction. He waved his arms and sent me on my way.

I knew immediately that I wanted to join the Central Bank when I met Patrick at my interview. Not that he said much. He sat back and let his colleague from Human Resources direct the interview. I have forgotten most of what took place that morning. But I do remember Patrick's questions. Or at least I remember how he asked them. Here was someone obviously incredibly thoughtful. His sense of humour, never far below the surface, was apparent. I did not necessarily want to work for the institution of the Central Bank. But I did want to work for Matthew and its Governor.

How full of myself must I have been at the age of 34 to believe I could make a difference in Dublin? At the time, this question did not occur to me, so it did not detain me. I suppose I answered it implicitly by taking the job. For the same hubristic reasons, I was pleased when the headline, 'Central Bank Employs Young Turk', appeared in a local financial services publication. My appointment to the role felt like a great compliment, and the press coverage was flattering. I was pleased to see my name in print. I liked being portrayed as a reformer. It matched my nascent self-image as the outsider coming to the rescue. It was all very exciting, intoxicating in fact, but I was a little naïve, and perhaps more confident than might be healthy for me. So it did me a lot of good when I realised the 'Young Turk' sobriquet would not cut much mustard at the Central Bank. I could sense the doubts among some of my new colleagues. And why would there not be doubts? In their eyes, I was new, and I was untested.

Not that there was much time to dwell on these arrival pains. Even before I joined the Central Bank, I had been drawn into the problems at Quinn Insurance. Two journalists, Gavin Daly and Ian Kehoe, described Sean Quinn's incredible rise and fall in *Citizen Quinn*. In 2009, I knew Sean Quinn had built a business worth billions through some well-judged, and equally well-executed, moves into different industries, including financial services. This final venture, Quinn Insurance, initially proved successful. It offered attractive prices, and so built market share quickly, especially in areas other insurers avoided, such as younger drivers. But in its quest for growth, it was pricing risk incorrectly, rendering its model unsustainable. Although this approach was true to Quinn's hard-nosed, entrepreneurial style, in financial services it brought him into direct conflict with the realities of regulation.

The Head of Insurance Supervision, Patrick Brady, had long suspected that all was not right at Quinn Insurance. His challenge had been to assemble the evidence needed to galvanise the Financial Regulator. Not that the situation was straightforward. As well as the problems at the insurance company, Sean Quinn had bought his way into Anglo Irish Bank through contracts for difference (CFDs) in Anglo's shares. These instruments did not give him a direct share in the bank, but they complicated an already messy situation. As Anglo imploded, the value of these contracts went into freefall. And in a twist symbolic of everything wrong with the Celtic Tiger, Sean Quinn had borrowed the money for the CFD purchases from Anglo. This created a complex web of relationships between the Quinn Group and Anglo Irish Bank which would take years to untangle.

What no one could prove was how indebted the Quinn Group was to Anglo. This would only be revealed later after forensic accountants had worked through its financial records. In 2010, the financial situation in the Quinn group was a mystery to outsiders. Consequently, no one knew for sure what might happen if Quinn Insurance fell over. Would other group companies follow? Only Sean Quinn and his closest associates understood the relationships between companies in the group. The Irish authorities and Anglo had, by comparison, very limited information. But the law was clear about the Central Bank's responsibilities. The insurance company had to meet regulatory requirements to continue trading.

But what would happen to the rest of the Quinn Group without the insurance company? And what would this mean for the repayment of its debts to the nationalised Anglo Irish Bank? The right decision on Quinn Insurance could easily lead to the wrong outcome for Anglo and, by extension, the Irish State. Was there a better example of the law of unintended consequences?

The Department of Finance certainly worried about these consequences, and asked that the pros and cons of appointing an administrator be weighed carefully. If the prospects of recovering debt from the Quinn Group worsened, this could affect the State's already fragile debt position. These choices were explored at length. As were the consequences for jobs at the Quinn Group. As was the issue of regulatory independence. But which was the most important? The government had very publicly made a virtue of regulatory independence. Could it now trade the reputation of the Central Bank and its new team against the highly uncertain prospect of repayment from the Quinn Group? The Minister of Finance, Brian Lenihan, listened to these arguments carefully.

While these issues were being discussed, new evidence emerged which suggested that the solvency position at Quinn Insurance was worse than first thought. The case to intervene was becoming more compelling as each day passed. Not that intervention would be straightforward. The existing legislation gave the Central Bank the power to act, but the available tools were blunt and inflexible. This left us scratching our heads. Surely there were more options to address the situation at Quinn? But there were not. The only answer was to ask a court to appoint an administrator. The main advantage of this approach was that the insurance company could be put on the right path. The main disadvantage was the lack of control. An administrator is accountable to the courts, not the Central Bank. This introduced unwanted uncertainty at a time when the stakes were high.

Yet if the stakes were high for decision-makers in the authorities, they were higher still for the employees. The politicians who visited the Central Bank in Dublin had brought employee representatives with them. There was no disputing Sean Quinn's record in creating meaningful jobs. So the potential loss of jobs, particularly after years of growth, was a shock to many associated with the Quinn Group. In moving testimony, the employees articulated their fears for the future. No one could argue that the situation looked bleak. But it was also clear that the Quinn Group's management had not levelled with the employee representatives. The employees had little understanding of the issues facing Quinn Insurance. This was not their fault. But someone should have told them what was happening before putting them in front of the Central Bank. Here was an early sign of how Sean Quinn was going to play his hand.

This was a misstep on Quinn's part as it misread the Central Bank's intentions. No one in the Irish authorities wanted to see Quinn Insurance fail. No one wanted to see job losses. Patrick Brady and his team worked tirelessly to find a future for the business. Increasingly this had to be done in the face of opposition from Cavan. None of this helped the group's employees. Much time and expense could have been avoided had Quinn cooperated. Instead he left to others to pick up the pieces.

Perhaps Quinn hoped the Central Bank was not serious. That it would back down. But this could not happen. The case was unarguable. The insurance company was breaking the law. The courts endorsed this judgement. On one level, this was an issue of regulatory independence. But once the courts were involved, it was about the rule of law. There was no compromise to be found on this point.

Yet there was no escaping the symbolism of this stand of principle. By the time the Quinn story broke, the media had already talked up Ireland's tougher regulatory regime. But it was only talk to that point. The action against Quinn Insurance provided proof that we were serious.

This mattered within Ireland given the collapse in confidence in the regulatory system. It also mattered outside Ireland, especially to those in EU capitals who had the potential to support the country's recovery. There was a view among some of these governments that Dublin has authored its own misfortune. That it had become a free-wheeling offshore centre where financial institutions could do as they pleased. The Central Bank's handling of Quinn Insurance had the potential to change this perception. To show it could put its house in order.

Not that this was ever a consideration in the decisions taken about Quinn Insurance in those months. The Central Bank acted to enforce insurance law. No more, no less. The courts endorsed this approach. Everything was done by the book. It was never a marginal call to seek the appointment of an administrator. But there can be no doubt that these decisions had a bearing on subsequent events in the financial crisis.

While all of this was going on, the storm clouds were gathering in financial markets, and a new term had been coined about Ireland, Greece, Portugal and Spain: the PIGS. Markets believed these countries were the weak links in the euro area chain, the countries least likely to be able to pay their debts. This was a different order of problem to those at Quinn Insurance. A problem with potentially existential consequences for the smallest of the PIGS.

Lesson #3: Imperfect decisions need to be made imperfectly.

On the afternoon of 18 July 1999, an improbable sporting outcome looked likely: a Frenchmen was a few swings away from winning the British Open golf championship. Jean Van de Velde needed only a six on the par four eighteenth hole at Carnoustie Golf Links to secure the title. It was a situation which called for composure. Instead, the Frenchman decided to launch a full frontal assault on the difficult final hole.

Using a driver from the tee, Van de Velde sent the ball wayward down the seventeenth fairway. Although safe, his first shot had left him some distance short of the eighteenth green, with a stream in between him and the hole. The textbook next shot, which almost every other player would have chosen, would have been a short iron to place his ball before the hazard. Instead, he pulled a two iron from his bag and sent the ball crashing into a stand full of spectators. Speaking after the event, Van de Velde said, 'I just didn't feel comfortable hitting a wedge. To me, it's against the spirit of the game, and maybe it would have been against the spirit of a Frenchman.'

It took Van de Velde another five shots to finish the hole. This put him in the play-offs, alongside two players who had finished on the same total score. Perhaps because the final hole had taken so much out of him, he could not sustain his challenge and had to watch Paul Lawrie lift the claret jug. The championship, which had been his to win, had slipped from his grasp in the agonising closing minutes of his final round.

Jean Van de Velde will not be alone in having replayed that final hole in his mind. We are drawn to examples of failure precisely because we want to understand what could have been different. There are lessons for life in these stories. And when we explore them we are learning much about crisis management.

On that July afternoon in 1999, the French golfer went through a crisis. He did things which changed the course of events. He did not do things which might have corrected this altered course and returned him to the path to victory. He failed, in other words, to manage his own crisis.

There are many accounts of that infamous afternoon in Scotland. They tend to focus on the actions Van de Velde could have taken, the clubs he could have drawn from his bag, the shots he could have made. This line of analysis is not incorrect, at least not in a narrow golfing sense. But it misses a key point. Van de Velde was not being logical or rational. He was not *thinking* as a golfer. He was *behaving* as someone with heightened emotions who happened to be playing golf. He suddenly ceased to apply those criteria which had governed his behaviour in the preceding rounds.

Anyone who is capable of putting themselves into such a changed state of mind is always going to find it hard to extract themselves, especially if their emotions are running high. Van de Velde did not realise he was in a crisis until it was too late. By that point he could not think himself back into a position of victory. As soon as he took his tee shot he was faced with a number of imperfect decisions, and then faced with having to make them in imperfect circumstances. He was unable to do so.

The ability to deal with changed circumstances is one factor which differentiates great athletes from the rest. How they respond to pressure. How they deal with setbacks. How clearly they see the situation in front of them. How aware they are of their own state of mind and that of an opponent. There is no question that raw physical ability and technique play a huge part in sporting success. But an athlete's state of mind, their mental ability and agility, is the true differentiating factor.

Something similar is true of leaders who prevail, perhaps even thrive, in a crisis. Not only are they able to see that the circumstances in which they are operating have changed. They find it within themselves to address these altered circumstances. In particular, they see quickly that continuing to do the same things, in the same way, will yield only the same results. They therefore change how things are done to suit the circumstances.

But changing how things are done is difficult, especially in large or complex organisations. It is difficult psychologically. Difficult to see that change is required, especially if things appear to be going well. Difficult to advocate a change of course, particularly if you are judged to be holding a minority or fringe opinion. It is much easier to drift with the tide, not to generate opposition, to work with the grain of the status quo. And these are some of the reasons why crises tend to get ahead of us before we get in front of them.

From an early age, we learn that doing things in a certain way is encouraged, while finding alternative ways of doing them is generally discouraged. This continues into adult life. One does not have to spend very long in a large organisation to understand that there is often pressure to conform to a certain way of doing things. This is useful where it allows organisations to function. There need to be commonly understood, repeatable processes. And this is fine until performing the process in the right way becomes more important than the outcome. Failed to fill in a form correctly? You don't get paid. Refused to follow the process to recruit someone? Lose the vacancy. This can have a debilitating effect on creativity and energy. It also drains an organisation of talent. As Rory Sutherland put it in his brilliant book, *Alchemy: The Surprising Power of Ideas that Don't Make Sense*, 'It is much easier to be fired for being illogical than it is for being unimaginative.'

Organisations can get away with the resulting bureaucracy and inertia when times are good. But in a crisis, when the tide goes out, the desire to do things 'in the right way' leaves the inflexible, rigid organisation floundering. For crisis management is an art, and art involves creativity. Creativity involves trial, error and mess, and it involves taking risks. No one knows precisely what they are doing in a crisis, nor is there a right way out of a crisis. It is an imperfect, imperfectible process. Or, as Leonard Cohen sang, 'Forget your perfect offering. There is a crack in everything.'

Yet there is always a way out of a crisis, as long as leaders learn through trial and error, make mistakes, and sometimes create a mess in finding the exit. Ireland escaped its crisis in a spectacularly messy fashion. But the nature of this success has not been much discussed in Ireland. Such accounts as do exist tend to be factual and, to my eyes at least, a little sombre. They overplay the importance of rational decision-making, and they underplay the random, ad hoc and emotionally charged nature of the crisis management effort. But perhaps this should not be surprising. There is, after all, an established way of accounting for crises, with most of this work done by economists. There are, of course, some magisterial accounts of crises written by economists. But they only ever tell part of the story.

One of the many paradoxes of Ireland's crisis is that there has been no official investigation into why the country recovered. Nor has there been a structured attempt to capture what it learned when doing so. There were a number of reports about the origins of the crisis, including one which emerged from parliamentary hearings which lasted longer than the crisis itself. But there is no official study of why the crisis resolution efforts of 2008 to 2012 worked. It is a paradox because the resolution of the crisis cost tens of billions of euros, thousands of jobs, many deaths and other unseen or unreported consequences. Lots of politicians asked how Ireland got into the mess. Not many have asked how it got out and whether it was worth it.

Such a study might provide a useful training manual for politicians and officials. It would show how little officials knew during the crisis. It would illustrate how little room for manoeuvre there was as it deepened. It would shed light on some of the self-limiting beliefs which influenced decisions. It would reveal the missed opportunities. It would also confirm two truths about crises. They are always a competition between least worst (imperfect) options. And in choosing between these options, imperfect decisions will be made imperfectly.

Nothing better illustrates these truths than the events which bookend the Irish crisis. On one side, in 2008, is the bank guarantee. On the other, in 2011, is the funding package agreed between the Troika and the Irish State. Both decisions were made under considerable pressure. Both were made from a weak negotiating position. Both were made with no insight into the future. Both were made in hope as much as expectation. Both were made in good faith. Both had a dramatic impact on Ireland's future. As examples of how decisions are made, there is actually little to distinguish them. Yet one, the guarantee, has been consistently vilified. The other, for the most part, celebrated.

Both were, of course, imperfect decisions taken imperfectly. The guarantee was a higher risk decision. Officials knew little about the banks. The implications for the Irish state were grave, even using cautious assumptions. In 2011, by contrast, officials had more information and more time. Yet even with these advantages, Ireland signed up to a support package which increased the national debt significantly. The whole point of the guarantee was to avoid incurring any liabilities. So which was the better decision? The answer depends on the frame of reference we apply to evaluate the decision.

Such a frame of reference needs to take account of the realities of decision-making in a crisis. And five things can be said in this regard. The first is there is an obligation to make choices, to decide. The second is that there is necessity, when making decisions, to choose between imperfect options. The third is to do so knowing, in a fast moving situation, where there is only imperfect information, that making decisions will itself be an imperfect process. The fourth is to accept that these decisions will be criticised. The fifth is to recognise the fourth lesson, take it into account, but not to let it stop decisions being made.

There may be a sixth lesson. The judgements made later about decisions taken in a crisis are themselves inherently imperfect. No one can be in the room retrospectively. No one can simulate the tension, recreate the fear, doubt and hesitation. No one can make the hairs stand on the back of their necks. Official reports are not history. They are a version of history, and often a slanted or partisan version at that.

At best, they are imperfect records of imperfect decisions taken imperfectly.

❄   ❄   ❄

The COVID-19 pandemic provides a fresh case study in imperfect decision making. Because it quickly became an existential issue for healthcare systems, there was an acceptance that decisions needed to be made quickly, and therefore mistakes were more likely. There was also a recognition among the public that because governments knew little about the virus, the official response would be imperfect. It took some months before this early acceptance of the challenges gave way to less forgiving assessments of governments, political leaders and officials.

There will be a long and drawn out process to evaluate what happened before and during the pandemic. This could be fruitful if it occurs in the right way and for the right reasons. But this does require an acceptance of the realities of crisis management – the six lessons I have identified already in this section. Should the crisis review processes become a means to attack individuals or institutions, they will serve little purpose. In fact they will do worse: we will miss an opportunity to be better prepared for the next crisis. We need to build more resilient systems, not dwell on the imperfections of the ones we had going into the crisis.

One source of greater resilience would be officials trained to make decisions in conditions of uncertainty. Governments are very good at selecting people on the basis of their assumed technical proficiency. They use very elaborate processes to select and appoint such people. But how often do governments ask whether someone might be up to the job when the shit hits the fan? Do we really train officials to deal with crises? Do governments actually have enough of those awkward people who ask whether enough is being done *before* a problem emerges?

One of my mentors, Michael Foot, a veteran of the Bank of England, once asked me to read the diary he kept during the collapse of Barings Bank. The failure of the British merchant bank in 1995 was a major event. Although Nick Leeson, the rogue trader, will forever be associated with its downfall, it is forgotten that an earthquake in Japan brought events to a head. Plunging Asian stock markets wiped out Leeson's positions. He fled Singapore for Malaysia, leaving the bank facing losses twice its available capital.

The Governor of the Bank of England, Sir Eddie George, asked Michael to sort out the mess. Michael's diary records the weeks after the bank's losses were known. Reading it is like watching someone solve a jigsaw puzzle where some pieces are blank, others are mis-shaped and many are missing. Michael's diary shows how, through bloody-minded determination, he eventually assembled a picture.

Michael asked me to read his diary after the 9/11 terrorist attacks. He realised that I needed help to understand how things work in a crisis. I have no doubt this helped, as did working with him in those months after the planes hit the Twin Towers and the Pentagon. The world felt like an uncertain and dangerous place, but with his guidance I came to see how it is possible to address the consequences of a crisis.

As we pass through the later phases of the COVID-19 crisis, we will continue to face uncertainty, and leaders will continue to have to make imperfect decisions. We need to accept that this is the reality of the complex world in which we live. There is much we have learned from the pandemic about our readiness, or otherwise, for future challenges. Even if we cannot be certain about the nature of these challenges, we can be certain we will face them.

Some lessons for leaders in a crisis:

1. **Understand the imperfect nature of imperfect information.** In a crisis, leaders are required to choose between options which are based on imperfect information. The process of making these choices will be itself inherently imperfect. And no one can foresee the consequences of a given option. Before making a decision, it is the leader's responsibility to understand the shortcomings of the process so they understand the risks of each option.

2. **Avoid analysis paralysis.** It is entirely legitimate for a leader to seek to improve the information available to them. But it is also incumbent on a leader to recognise the difference between a genuine search for information and prevarication. Analysis paralysis is common in government and business. In a crisis, it can waste valuable time. A leader needs to prevent its spread.

3. **Don't look over your shoulder.** It is inevitable that decisions taken in a crisis will be reviewed in the future. This thought can be debilitating and distracting, often at the very moment when key decisions need to be made. As long as a leader can say, hand on heart, they sought to make the best possible decision, and did so in good faith, there is not much more that can be done. As the philosopher, Søren Kierkegaard, said, 'Life can only be understood backwards; but it must be lived forwards'.

4.

Repairing a Central Bank

The rattle of the Central Bank's executive tea trolley signalled the arrival of mid-morning on the deep carpeted seventh floor of Dame Street. It was always admirably punctual. Well stocked with biscuits, and adorned by fine bone china crockery, it could have rolled off the set of Downton Abbey.

Perhaps the tea trolley was a harmless perk. Perhaps it saved time waiting for a kettle to boil. But in 2010, it felt out of place. It was a relic. A relic of a culture in which privileged executives, unlike everyone else, had tea and coffee brought to them. A culture which placed too much emphasis on hierarchy. A culture which, at times, seemed to confuse an individual's position on a structure chart with their contribution and relevance. Needless to say, none of this was the fault of the tea trolley. It never stopped anyone doing, thinking or saying anything. But it symbolised much of what was problematic and unhealthy in the Central Bank's culture.

The tea trolley's abolition was therefore necessary, if not universally popular. It was one of many changes needed to overcome a pervasive, and disabling, deference at Dame Street. Its traces were everywhere when I arrived at the Central Bank. In memos. In meetings. In the allocation of car parking spaces. In the thickness of the carpets on different floors. In the way more junior colleagues addressed senior colleagues. In the way senior colleagues talked to junior ones. In the allocation of offices. In the tea trolley. None of this would have mattered had the Central Bank performed well during before and during the crisis. But it had not.

This had to change for its own sake. It also had to change as we had a crisis to manage, and a deferential culture is not one in which bad news travels fast, if it travels at all. In a deferential culture, employees tend to become concerned about looking good in the eyes of superiors, or at least not looking bad or being found out. If success is defined in these terms, why bother to challenge decisions which roll down the organisational mountain? Why send things back up the chain of command if they might make your boss look bad? A determined, open leader can overcome some of these con-straints. Such a leader might even be able to encourage open expression. But this takes a lot of time, especially if colleagues have become used to a certain way of doing things. Or if they have found hiding places. But when people hide, you can be sure the issues you need to know about are hiding too.

But how to modernise an institution in the eye of a storm? How to invigorate a central bank which had steadily lost power and influence over many decades? And how to take a group of people on this journey who had got used to a certain way of doing things? The crisis was, of course, incom-parable in Irish financial history. There had been economic downturns, and periodic blow-ups in the financial sector, since the Central Bank's foundation in 1943. But these were all manageable. It had therefore entered the global financial crisis far from battle-ready.

It did not help that the Central Bank had been steadily hollowed-out in the 2000s. Ireland's membership of the euro had reduced Dame Street's influence and authority. Monetary policy, one of the most important activities a central bank can undertake, was decided in Frankfurt when Ireland joined the euro. For ambitious central bankers, attractive and important jobs became available at the European Central Bank (ECB).

The EU's growing role in financial services also had an impact. Like every other EU member state, Ireland increasingly became a rule taker rather than a rule setter. Not only did this mean that policy was outsourced. It also meant more time was spent checking compliance with these EU-wide rules rather than supervising the risks in financial institutions.

This inheritance meant the Central Bank needed a new purpose. It would not be enough to equip it with new powers and resources. It needed a new story about its important role in Ireland, and some fire in its belly. It also needed a new story so the narrative of regulatory failure could be consigned to history. In particular, there was a need to expunge any perception that the Central Bank would again defer to industry or politicians. And this was the opportunity for the new leadership team. Although we could not repatriate powers from Frankfurt or Brussels, we could act with independence and a sense of purpose.

Many of the issues of regulatory culture and practice were examined in the report which the government commissioned Patrick Honohan to write about the crisis. Published in May 2010, this became our blueprint for reform. He artfully diagnosed the causes of the crisis. He described the role the Central Bank had played. He was careful not to apportion blame or single out individuals for criticism. But he did make it clear what had gone wrong, and what needed to change. Although this was in some respects self-evident, the report provided the new team at the Central Bank with further reasons to do things differently.

But there was no disguising the fact the Central Bank and some of its employees were damaged. Dame Street, and some of its officials, had been under attack for nearly three years. The generalised criticism was bad enough. To make it worse, some officials had been named publicly. For people already dealing with guilt and related emotions, this public shaming could not have come at a worse time. There were teams in Dame Street experiencing a form of battle fatigue, and individuals suffering from stress. It was not a healthy organisation.

The arrival of a new leadership team risked adding to these pressures. No one could know how the outsiders would treat them. Everyone could see that Patrick Honohan and Matthew Elderfield were being held up as potential saviours. But how ruthless might they be in pursuit of reform? Psychological safety is important for humans. It matters especially in adversity. I have no doubt the Central Bank did not feel like a safe place for some people at that time. So while there was endless public discussion about stresses and strains in the economy, there was little attention given to the equivalent challenges facing individuals battered by events. In their own way, these issues were as intractable as those in the financial system.

Matthew and I talked at length about the individuals we believed were most affected by the crisis. We could see the damage first-hand. And although we did not state our objective in these terms, our instinct was to do no harm. There were no dismissals. No one was hung out to dry. There was no scapegoating. We wanted to protect those most exposed.

But we also had to bring about change. A rallying call was needed. Most of our new colleagues had not suffered directly themselves. But they had seen others suffer, and they had been working for an organisation criticised regularly. We therefore needed to restore their confidence and pride. We also needed to create a more dynamic and open way of working. We were, after all, still in a crisis. This required us to find people willing to implement the recommendations in Patrick's report.

This was important as Patrick's report would only have an impact if its recommendations became part of the Central Bank's day-to-day work. While he had identified a number of specific actions to be taken, his overriding concern was that there be a far-reaching change in the culture of regulation. This meant, by definition, the regulator had to change. So we needed to be clear about where we wanted to go.

I had seen this done before, and I thought it was straightforward enough. Or so I told myself when, with help from the knowledgeable and thoughtful Mary Burke, I started to write 'Banking Supervision: Our New Approach'. The main objective was to create a fresh narrative about the Central Bank's role in the economy and society. I hoped that by establishing this connection to a higher purpose we could achieve a number of objectives. For a start, I wanted the document to inspire our people, to make it clear why their work mattered. For this reason, I wanted us to be bold, to do things which mattered.

'Our New Approach' was not only designed to bring about change, it was also designed to send a very clear signal to the outside world that we had changed. This meant we had to engage the media. *The Financial Times* and *Wall Street Journal* both ran favourable stories. RTÉ, the national broadcaster, led with our publication on its six o'clock television news programme. David Murphy, the station's business editor, had interviewed me for his report earlier in the day. It was strange to see myself on television, and stranger still for my daughter to see her father following the Angelus.

Common to the coverage as a whole was the clear message that things were going to be different at the Central Bank and, therefore, different for banks. The word 'intrusive' featured in a few headlines. I was encouraged that international publications were willing to write a positive story about Ireland. We had taken a lot of care to brief them. We wanted them to know that we were serious.

'Banking Supervision' created the platform we needed to reform the Central Bank and, even more ambitiously, the banking system. But it was only a platform. The delivery of our plans was always going to depend on appointing the right leaders and managers. And this mattered, particularly in 2010. The organisation was growing. It was reforming itself. And we were still in the midst of a crisis which looked likely to get worse. We therefore had to identify those leaders who could realise the vision we had set out in 'Our New Approach'. Fortunately, the Central Bank already contained people eager and, more importantly, able to make a difference. The challenge was to ensure they were in the right roles so change would happen.

The priority area was banking supervision. This team had experienced the full force of the crisis. There was an urgent need to inject new energy and ideas. After some months of getting to know the team, I was in a better position to see where these qualities might come from.

To bolster its resources, the Central Bank had already recruited new people with experience gained in banks. Although their knowledge of regulation had come from being on the receiving end, this did not matter. Of these outsiders, Shane O'Neill, Michael Feeney and Dermot Monaghan stood out. All of them knew what had really gone on inside the banks. Michael Feeney in particular had a deep understanding of banking practices in the Celtic Tiger years. He knew where to look for problems. Dermot and Shane were very comfortable with the calculations required to stress test the banks' capital estimates. They also understood the problems lurking in the banks' loan books. Complementing this collection of outsiders was a talented cohort of longer serving Central Bank employees. Of this group, Dwayne Price was the stand out figure. Like Shane, Michael and Dermot, Dwayne was unafraid of fresh ideas and new ways of doing things. Like them, he also wanted to sort out the mess in his country.

The final member of this group of reformers was the last to join the Central Bank, John Moran. The irrepressible Limerick man had decided it was his duty to save his country even before he returned to Ireland. He had been living in France when he wrote to Patrick and offered his services. He arrived at Dame Street for an introductory meeting full of energy and ideas. I could tell he was a little bemused at the prospect of reporting to two Englishmen in the middle of an Irish crisis, but he kept this to himself. He got stuck into his new role supervising international banks in Ireland immediately, galvanising a team at some risk of being the poor relation to domestic banking supervision. He later took this same energy into his work on the future of the banking system.

This team had many qualities, but it was not one blessed by small personalities and inconsequential egos. It may not have been able to work together easily in peacetime conditions, but what unsuited them to normal regulatory work made them perfect in a crisis. Perhaps because they were too busy to compete, they found a way to work with one another. More importantly, they were comfortable moving at pace, demanding the same of others, and pressing hard for results.

They were also resilient and adept at learning from setbacks. This was just as well. For as 2010 wore on, things were increasingly difficult for the Irish State and Irish banks.

Lesson #4: People who agree with you are not always helping.

Following the Battle of Jutland in 1917, where the British fleet had performed poorly against its German adversary, the First Lord of the Admiralty passed a withering judgement on Admiral Jellicoe: 'He has all the qualities of Nelson bar one: he does not know how to disobey!'

During a crisis it is essential to have people willing and able to disagree with their leaders and colleagues. Decisions on significant issues, made at speed, are inherently risky. They need to be challenged if they are to be improved. This means having people in the room who have thought about the issues from first principles. It also means having people willing to give their perspective. A mute sage is of little use in a crisis. The challenge is to find the people able to contribute.

I have always enjoyed working with people who are happy to challenge those in authority. People who are comfortable with disagreement. Such people tend to be curious and, as Egon Zehnder demonstrated in research published in the *Harvard Business Review*, curiosity is a strong predictor of leadership potential. And as we have seen again during the pandemic, a crisis turns on the decisions leaders make. Constructive curiosity, when it leads to better answers, is gold dust in a crisis.

The point about ideas is that they do not get better as a consequence of hierarchy. If no one is willing to step outside the hierarchy, to put aside role and status, ideas are either not conceived at all or weighed on how they will come across to the most senior person in the room. As well as curtailing innovation and decision-making, putting hierarchy first sucks the energy from teams and organisations. Hierarchy and discipline are important to execution. But *executing* the right thing is essential to execution. A determination of the 'right thing' can only emerge from debate, discussion and unfettered thinking.

This is why central banks and regulators need disagreeable people. People who are more interested in finding the right answers than accepting prevailing wisdoms. Such people do not fit naturally into the rigid structures which bureaucracies prefer. Nor do they thrive in those cultures. So an extra effort has to be made to find them a home. The Irish authorities, particularly the Central Bank, were fortunate to attract enough of these right people at the right time. They made all the difference, even if they could be difficult colleagues.

Not, of course, that this archetype is a new one. The Greek philosopher, Socrates, encouraged his pupils to find themselves by thinking for themselves. In modern business, Thomas J Watson, the founder of IBM, said, 'don't make friends who are comfortable to be with. Make friends who will force you to lever yourself up'. The writer, Michael Lewis, has celebrated the awkward, questioning misfit in a number of books, notably *Moneyball* and *The Big Short*.

The challenge with such people is that they do not tend to fit in anywhere. It is not in their nature to be agreeable, to follow the rules and processes which their colleagues attempt to wrap around them. This is a real problem for regulators as they have come to fetishise the concept of 'challenge' within financial institutions. Junior regulators are sent out to look for examples of 'challenge' as a traffic warden might be dispatched to identify motoring violations. I understand why this happens, but it has the unintended consequence of turning what should be a beneficial activity – creative, expansive discussion of alternative futures – into a process of painting-by-numbers. And creative, disagreeable people do not like to paint by numbers.

In modern organisations, strategy and risk functions are supposed to perform this work. It is their job, at least in theory, to imagine alternative futures and present them for consideration. But the process expectations we have layered onto organisations have had two negative effects. They have created hiding places for organisations who, although they lack an ability or appetite to confront alternative futures, nonetheless possess a facility to make a process look really good. And they have led to an elaborate game of cat and mouse, whereby most of a risk team's time and effort goes into aligning risk processes with some mythical best practice or golden standard.

This obsession with process has a bedfellow in an insistence on formality. We know that many invaluable discussions often occur informally outside formal settings. And why wouldn't they? We are more likely to be open to ideas when we are relaxed, as we are more likely to share ideas when our words are not being recorded. But this is not what happens. The entire edifice of corporate governance has been constructed on the creation of artificial encounters. Not only is this all rather pointless, but it gets in the way of those difficult conversations which can prevent crises, or those creative conversations which can lead to greater preparedness for future challenges.

❄   ❄   ❄

We will soon learn about the difficult conversations which did not happen before the pandemic, or at least did not happen in the right way. The focus, inevitably, will fall on the decisions themselves. What governments and officials did or did not do. The options they considered, the ones they adopted, those they discounted. Individuals will emerge who claim they were ignored or overruled, their evidence and suggestions overlooked. The world will sit in judgement, but forget that while hindsight can help us see a great deal, it does not mean we will see things clearly.

But this will not stop many from engaging in a contest to be right after the event. This discourse will generate more heat than light, more opinions than answers. It will expose the uncomfortable truth that our desire to understand things is often less important to us than it is to be right. We can only ever see through a glass darkly, whether we are looking forward or back. And one reason for the darkness is that we find it hard to come at the world with an open, enquiring mind.

The irony, of course, is that arguments about the pandemic will involve deep disagreement. Having earlier been too agreeable to see the open stable, there will be no limit to our appetite to be disagreeable about the absent horse. The American writer, Gore Vidal, was on to something when he said, 'The four most beautiful words in our common language: I told you so'.

Instead, we need to pay attention to the facts. We need to take time to discover why things did not happen. In other words, we should use the crisis to understand how we might improve how we make decisions. Lots of questions suggest themselves. Was something like the COVID-19 outbreak considered so unlikely that we made precious few preparations? Had anyone thought through how a lockdown could be managed to minimise its social and economic impact? Why were some countries so much better than others at implementing testing regimes? These and many other questions will be asked about the inadequacy of contingency plans. And there will, inevitably, be many who want to know who was asking the difficult questions inside government.

But more fundamentally, what do the answers tell us about how governments operate? There was nothing inevitable about the global financial crisis, yet it happened. There was nothing inevitable about the weaknesses of the banks before the crisis struck, yet they existed. Similarly, governments have been considering pandemic scenarios for years, yet the defences were self-evidently inadequate. The question of what we did not do is important, but *why* we did not do the right things will be more revealing. Only then can we join the dots between events, and only then will we know whether there is something fundamentally problematic in public administration, in how we are governed.

The instinct to ask 'why' is also preventative. But it often induces headwinds, often finds resistance. Fewer ships sank due to overloading after Samuel Plimsoll, the British MP, asked why a line should not be drawn around a ship's hull to mark its safe draught. But it took him years to overcome the opposition of shipowners in Parliament. When C. Hunter Sheldon, a Californian neurosurgeon, asked why he was seeing so many head injuries following car accidents, Congress passed the National Traffic and Motor Vehicle Safety Act, leading to improved safety standards. But this was eleven years after Hunter published his study, and it involved a long struggle by activists against the automobile industry.

The COVID-19 crisis is a stark illustration of why we need to ask 'why'. But are governments disposed to take the long view? Are they organised to deal with complex uncertainties decades from now? Are those hierarchical structures in public administration amenable to constructive disagreement? Or is top-down managerialism likely to snuff out those discussions which might improve our collective resilience? We need to know the answers so that our governments can be fit for purpose.

And being 'fit for purpose' means having a voice inside any organisation willing and able to challenge prevailing orthodoxies. That voice which will advocate alternative courses of action, describe other possible scenarios. That voice which might be asking right now what we will do if something worse than COVID-19 comes along. Which will be asking how we manage the consequences of higher levels of government debt. The voice of those people who will be thinking about how we fight the next major crisis.

Who will not, in other words, be a voice simply agreeing with the people around them.

Some lessons for leaders in a crisis:

1. **The search for better answers never ends.** It is the leader's responsibility to find the best answers to the challenges they face. It is not about being right. It is not about pleasing others. It is not about having solutions which look great. It is the leader's job in a crisis to role model the unending search for better questions and, therefore, better answers.

2. **Keep the doers and thinkers, lose the talkers.** Leaders will be surrounded by three types of individual. Thinking people. Doing people. And people who talk about thinking and doing. They need to dispense with the third type and create a balanced team of the first and second.

3. **Manage the valuable distractions**. A thinking, questioning individual can be a leader's best ally. Leaders need someone who will tell them the uncomfortable truths. But as they can become a distraction, it is the leader's job to find a way to channel the energy of this valuable colleague, not to demotivate them by cutting short discussions or excluding them.

5.

Failing a Way to Success

Matthew put his head in his hands. 'This could blow a hole in our stress test. It could be very damaging.'

The European Banking Authority (EBA) had just announced its own stress test, only weeks after the Irish test had been published on 30 March. Patrick sighed, looked towards Shane O'Neill, and asked him what we knew about the assumptions the EBA was proposing to use. Shane said he thought the EBA's parameters would be in line with our own. Even so, the risk that Irish banks could fail the EBA test was real. We groaned.

By early summer, 2010 was proving to be a difficult year. The Irish authorities had worked hard, against the odds, to break the link between the banks and the Irish State. The country was fighting to retain credibility in financial markets so it could borrow. With the announcement of a new, Europe-wide stress test, it suddenly felt like this work might be for nothing. Was the EU intent on making Ireland's problems worse?

The year had not started this way. There had been grounds for optimism. There was a new leadership team at the Central Bank. Ireland's 'bad bank', the National Asset Management

Agency (NAMA), was up and running. Some of the banks, including Anglo Irish, had new management. There was hope that the world's major economies were through the worst of the global financial crisis. No one at the Central Bank was sanguine about the depth of the problems at the banks. Nor did we look at the public finances through rose-tinted spectacles. But it was not a given that things would get worse.

The decision to conduct an Irish stress test in March 2010 was about making things better. By then a number of countries had completed stress tests, including the UK and US in 2009. The theory behind these exercises was straightforward enough. During the global financial crisis, doubts about the financial strength of individual banks had heightened fear and uncertainty. For creditors to have confidence in banks, they needed to be sure they were financially sound, and not just sound at a point in time but sound for years to come. Proponents of stress tests argued that they were an effective way to demonstrate the risks which existed in individual banks and in the banking system as a whole. The alternative, they argued, was endless speculation in the absence of reliable information.

Certainly the exercises in Japan, the UK and US seemed to have gone some way to restoring confidence in the banking systems of those countries. But was this because of the stress tests? Or was it because each country could afford to support its banks? The answers to these questions mattered a great deal. It would be easy to construct an exercise in Ireland which replicated the tests in other countries. It would not be possible to replicate the context in which these tests had taken place. For a start, the amount of Irish bank debt relative to national output (a measure of debt sustainability) exceeded the equivalent ratios in the UK and US. Ireland also had fewer economic 'shock absorbers' than London or Washington. It did not have its own currency. Monetary policy was decided in Frankfurt. Dublin was also committed to euro area fiscal rules. So whereas the UK and US could pursue inflationary (or, at least, counter-deflationary) solutions, Dublin could not print money to take care of its debt burden. Until the euro area embraced the sort of expansionary policies pursued in Britain, Japan or the US, Ireland was left to face into a deflationary future.

The inability to replicate the conditions in non-euro area countries, or at least to narrow the differences, was one argument against an Irish stress test. There were others. One obvious objection was that an exercise designed to reduce uncertainty could have the opposite effect, triggering the event – a bank failure – it was designed to discourage. Since this is an acknowledged drawback of stress tests, critics argue that it is consequently very hard to run tests in which banks fail. There is a temptation for regulators to moderate their demands of banks. When this happens the validity of a test is inevitably questioned. The same risk arises where the amount of capital a bank has to raise following a stress test is too great. These were precisely the dilemmas the Central Bank faced in 2010. What amount of capital would be convincing? What could the banks afford? What amount might put the government's finances at risk? Such trade-offs were unattractive, but they could not be avoided. Ireland did not have inexhaustible resources at its disposal.

But if going ahead with the stress test was risky, cancelling it was unappealing. Here was another argument against stress tests. Once a test is announced, it is almost impossible to change course. The market's expectations are raised. The media, attracted by the simple binary (pass or fail) nature of a test, turns the results announcement into a sort of negative awards ceremony, with winning and losing banks named and shamed. It was not unreasonable to ask, as some did, whether this made the banking system safer. But as the crisis dragged on, it was becoming harder for regulators and central banks to resist demands for these tests. A sort of stress test arms race developed. There was also an insatiable appetite from markets for transparency, for ever more detail about the data and assumptions regulators were using. But where to begin and where to end the accompanying disclosures? There was no right answer.

To complicate matters in Dublin, or at least to add to the drama of the occasion, there was a test within the stress test. The arrival of Patrick and Matthew had started to convince critics that perhaps the Central Bank could get a grip on the banking crisis. But could Patrick and Matthew sort out the banks? It remained a mammoth task. The stress test was also a public examination of the new Governor and his team.

For a time it looked like the Central Bank might have passed. But the problem with banking crises is that it can take more than one attempt to locate the bottom. Things that one would prefer to know beforehand only reveal themselves later. In March 2010, the gap in our knowledge was the timing of loan transfers to NAMA. To get around the fact that NAMA was still in the early stages of placing a value on loans moving from the banks, we had to make some assumptions about future values. These were sound in theory. In practice, they proved to be way off the mark.

When the final NAMA transfers were confirmed later in the year, the stress test results had to be updated to reflect much steeper discounts. This forced the banks to seek further capital injections.

But to write this as a story of Irish failure would be unfair and inaccurate, even though this is how it was portrayed at the time. I can vividly recall the comment of one former senior UK regulator who chided the Irish authorities for, in her words, 'fucking up Europe'. As well as being hyperbolic, this comment betrayed a surprising lack of understanding about what had happened in Dublin. We were not doing too little. We were trying to do too much. Otherwise sensible policies were colliding. Ireland was not the first country to experiment with bad banks and stress tests. But the Irish State did not have enough money to pay for them.

This became all too apparent during 2010. The price of Irish government debt fell as markets began to doubt the Irish State's ability (or willingness) to honour its obligations. It was like watching the pulse line drop on a heart rate monitor. A flat line would, in financial terms, indicate default. As this moment approached, there appeared to be nowhere left to turn, no policies left to try, no more shots in the locker. Everything seemed to point towards this outcome.

This was certainly the fear among policy makers in Dublin. We discussed it at length behind closed doors. Our problem, however, was that the markets and media were discussing sovereign default openly. The possibility of Greece renouncing its debt was a recurring headline. But as no euro area government has ever defaulted on euro denominated debt, how realistic were these fears? The market was increasingly of the view they were very real. Many were sceptical that Greece, Ireland and Portugal (and possibly others) could survive without some reduction in their total debt. Friends and contacts in the UK and Europe asked me when I thought Ireland would default. It seemed everyone thought it was a matter of *when*, not *if*.

The source of this turmoil was fear about the integrity of the euro area: whether the euro would survive. The failed stress test may not have been a great advertisement for Irish policymakers, but the government in Dublin could hardly be blamed for seeking bold and innovative ways out of the crisis. That it could not afford to escape was hardly a reason to criticise Irish officials. Dublin's problems were euro area problems, requiring euro area solutions.

The Irish crisis was one part of a larger crisis in the euro area. It was a story of dangerous imbalances between the economies of the currency union. That the euro area's policymakers did not acknowledge this openly did not mean it was untrue. But Athens, Dublin and Lisbon were trapped. Trapped inside a chamber which, unless the pressures were released, would crush them or force them to float free.

So a way of reducing the debts of these countries had to be found. Or they had to be restructured to be manageable. But what did debt reduction mean in the euro area? No one knew. Did it mean Ireland walking away from its debts? Not according to other euro area governments. Did it mean the euro area coming to Ireland's rescue? Again, there was nothing to suggest Ireland's partners would grasp this nettle. Markets spotted this dead end and Irish government bond yields rose further. This put more pressure on the State, further reducing its policy choices. The compression chamber was becoming ever more uncomfortable. But it was not obvious that anyone was coming to Ireland's rescue.

Markets sensed that euro area governments were running for cover. No country wanted its financial institutions to be the last ones holding Greek, Irish or Portuguese debt. This led Ireland's euro area partners to insist it honour its own guarantee for all categories of debt, including the highest risk tranches. This was as bold as it was cynical. Every euro which left Dublin was one less for a French or German bank or taxpayer to have to find should Ireland default. It looked very much like national interests were taking priority over those of the euro area as a whole. This added to a growing sense that the euro area did not have a plan or, worse, that a game of last man standing was underway. The dream of those who designed the euro risked turning into a nightmare. No one seemed to be in charge, perhaps because no one was in charge.

The absence of mutuality in the euro area at this pivotal moment contrasted with what had happened when everything was going well. Banks across Europe had benefited from the expansion of Irish banks' balance sheets in the 2000s. But when funding for the Irish banks started to dry up from 2007, they were left facing a terrifying mismatch between what they had borrowed and what they had lent. But now that the Irish banks were in deep trouble, there were precious view banks ready to plug the gap.

This should not have been an unmanageable problem. The banks had access to funds through the euro area's lender of last resort, the ECB. One of the core purposes of a central bank is to lend to banks when they cannot borrow from other sources. The Bank of England, US Federal Reserve and other central banks had done exactly this during the global financial crisis. For a time, the ECB did the same. But then it hesitated. Soon afterwards it started to insist on certain conditions being met before it would continue to lend. Then it began to ask for its money back. It was as if a lifeboat, in sight of the sinking ship, had turned tail. This did nothing to calm financial markets. It exacerbated an already difficult situation in Dublin. But why did it happen?

The ECB is unlike most central banks. Almost all central banks are extensions of a national government. The Bank of England was created to help the British government fund its wars in Europe. The US Federal Reserve system emerged from 1791 in response to the changing financial needs of the Federal Government. The relationship between governments and central banks makes them unlike every other bank.

Since governments and central banks are entwined, most governments guarantee unconditionally the liabilities of the national central bank. A central bank cannot be allowed to fail. For this reason, taxpayers effectively stand behind central banks. And in an extreme scenario, where a government or central bank created liabilities which taxpayers could not, or would not wish to, fund, there is an option for the central bank to print money to pay the costs.

The ECB is different. Its solvency is not guaranteed by a single state. In theory, the members of the euro area stand behind the ECB. But the euro area is not a nation state (as was increasingly apparent as the crisis dragged on). During the crisis, this had a number of implications for the ECB. When it acted as the lender of last resort, there was some doubt about exactly who stood behind its loans. To complicate matters, each member of the single currency had its own political priorities. Whereas the UK government could support a Scottish bank using tax revenues from England (and vice versa), the German government could not easily do the same for a Greek bank. Consequently, whereas the Bank of England could lend to RBS without having to worry about losing money if it were to collapse, the ECB was far less sure of the security of its position in a Greek bank. The crisis was not only testing the theory of a currency union, it was testing the practice of central banking in a currency union – a currency union which appeared, in some fundamental ways, to be incomplete.

For the ECB to be able to function like a normal central bank, it needed to be confident that euro area governments would protect its balance sheet. The ECB could not resolve this question on its own. It required the euro area's governments to have a common view of the ECB's role. Was it to be an interventionist central bank or not? Given the ECB's exposure to weak banks, it also required these governments to have a common understanding about *how* losses would be shared. In 2010 it was unable to agree *whether* they would be shared. This left the ECB unable to fight the crisis. Its hesitancy was evident to anyone following events.

The loans the ECB had already made to Irish banks shed some light on its predicament. The money it advanced to local banks in the euro area passed through national central banks. The national central banks, in turn, lent this money to local banks. Under this arrangement, any losses in a default would fall on the ECB since the national central bank had a claim on its balance sheet. But there was a second category of central bank funding, Emergency Liquidity Assistance (ELA). Designed to be a short-term source of funding, ELA could be advanced at the discretion of a national central bank. Unlike normal eurosystem funding, the risk of ELA sat on a national central bank's balance sheet, not the ECB's. For various reasons, including the conduct of monetary policy, the ECB had to approve ELA, or at least not object to its use.

There were a few problems with ELA in an Irish context. Because the risk sat with the Central Bank, it was, in effect, considered a claim on the government. Or, to be more precise, it might end up being a claim in certain circumstances. The Irish government was certainly not willing to be drawn on this point. And as the amount of ELA increased, the attraction of constructive ambiguity grew.

It did not help that ELA was more expensive than normal eurosystem funding. This justifiably irked the Department of Finance. As the ECB would not make eurosystem funding available when banks ran out of eligible collateral, Irish banks had to rely more and more on ELA. Anglo Irish was funded almost exclusively by ELA. This drove up the costs for the banks and the Irish State. A perception developed in markets that ELA was not as good as normal eurosystem funding. This did nothing to help the Irish cause.

ELA became a bellwether for the euro area's difficulties. My colleagues who worked most closely with Frankfurt were adamant that the distinction between ELA and eurosystem funding made sense. It struck me as largely artificial. It also seemed to be precisely the sort of quasi-theological, hair-splitting point about which central bankers enjoy obsessing. The Irish banks needed cheap and plentiful funding. ELA was not the right answer.

As I saw it, either the euro area would stand together or it would not. ELA undercut the principle of loss sharing. It therefore undermined the euro area. Who would recapitalise a national central bank if there were a default on ELA? What would the ECB do if one of its constituent central banks failed? Would the euro area stand behind the ECB in the event it made good losses on ELA? To its critics, ELA was another example of the euro area's design flaws.

There is a darker interpretation of the ECB's actions in this period, which suggests that political rather than economic considerations drove its response to the crisis. The central charge is that Frankfurt acted under instructions from the euro area's larger governments. Banks in Germany and France were certainly heavily exposed to Greece and Ireland. The ECB's insistence, early in the crisis, that banks should repay all creditors benefited financial institutions elsewhere in the euro area. This made life harder for Greece, Ireland and Portugal. None of this proves that larger countries controlled or coerced the ECB. Nor does it prove, if there was such pressure, that the ECB acquiesced. Yet neither does it disprove the charge. There has never been a completely satisfactory explanation as to why the ECB believed it to be right that private sector creditors should be protected by taxpayers. That it later allowed depositors to suffer losses in Cyprus only adds to the need for a comprehensive account of its policy in this period.

But there are a few problems with this line of attack. The first is that the ECB was undoubtedly making policy on the hoof. Although central banks tend to be shrouded in mystery, and the language central bankers use obscure and indirect, they are neither omniscient nor omnipotent. This was certainly true of the ECB in 2010. Furthermore, it was still a young institution. Its officials had little experience of crisis management. They may have worked for an institution that looked like a central bank, but it was not a normal central bank in ways which clearly affected its handling of the crisis. The most plausible explanation of its stance is that it feared that as soon as one country restructured liabilities, others would follow. As this would undoubtedly have made the crisis worse, and quite possibly have fractured the currency union irrevocably, its insistence on full repayment makes some sense. The ECB did not choose to sit on a political faultline, and its actions have to be judged accordingly.

While the ECB was navigating this difficult terrain, the clock was ticking in Dublin. Not that Ireland was alone. The problems of Greek and Portuguese banks were well known. There were also doubts about the health of banks in Spain and Italy. Weak to non-existent economic growth in the euro area was causing some to question whether the problems might be more widespread. In the absence of the sort of bold, calming measures pursued in the UK and US, pressure built in the euro area for more transparency about the health of banks. The arguments which had led Ireland towards its stress test now started to attract advocates in the ECB and European capitals. Momentum started to build behind the idea that something needed to be done to restore confidence.

The favoured 'something' was, again, to be a stress test. But how could a central bank with no powers to supervise banks deliver such a test? Banking supervision remained a national responsibility in the euro area. At the same time, the ECB wanted to avoid a euro area-only test. Although it was plain that many of the problems were in the euro area, the ECB feared that a test focused exclusively on the currency union would reinforce negative perceptions of the euro area. This said much about the ECB's state of mind at the time.

For these and other reasons, the European Banking Authority (EBA) was asked to deliver the exercise for the EU as a whole. The EBA comprised heads of banking supervision from EU Member States. It had been created to bring together the EU's banking regulators and coordinate its regulations. In simple terms, it existed to encourage harmonisation across the European Single Market. It was not designed to deal with individual bank issues. Nor was it resourced to deliver a stress test. But it was the only EU-wide entity capable of delivering what the ECB and certain EU member states wanted.

Like most EU groups, the EBA was large and unwieldy. It also contained unofficial subdivisions. It naturally divided between euro area members and the rest. There was a distinction between regulators who sat outside a central bank and those, as in Ireland, where the central bank's responsibilities included banking regulation. There were then those regional blocs who aligned as much for cultural as policy reasons. The most notable of these groups were the Scandinavians and Eastern Europeans. The most important division, however, was the less obvious one between those countries able to support their banks and everyone else. Such a split could hardly be surprising in an economy as large as the EU. But it was one which mattered.

The EBA was going to have to perform its stress test in full knowledge of these divisions. It was also going to do so after a number of Europe's governments had reiterated publicly their objections to EU-wide loss sharing. This was not the best start for the EBA. Andrea Enria, the EBA's cerebral chairman, knew their credibility was at stake. Everyone around the EBA table knew the stronger countries would need to support weaker ones if the crisis were to end. But there was no plan for this to happen. As with the earlier Irish stress test, the EBA exercise would occur without a euro area solution for its damaged banks.

As those sceptical of the EBA had forecast, the results disappointed. Critics were quick to pounce on the fact that only seven banks of ninety failed. Either the test had not made enough demands of banks, they argued, or some countries had fiddled the results. The outcome also implied that senior people in the EU were in denial about the problems facing Europe's banks. If this were the case, market participants reasoned, the same people were hardly likely to address these problems. If they were not in denial, and the stress test was the best Europe could offer, there was every chance the problems would get worse.

There was some hope that the EBA's test would force the ECB to be more accommodating. This was certainly our hope in Dublin. If more problems came to the surface, we reasoned, it would be harder for Frankfurt to sit on its hands. This did not happen. The ECB's bullish statement welcoming the results confirmed it was happy to see the can kicked further down the road. None of this was EBA's fault. But its stress test had also fallen short.

Or so it seemed at the time. The truth was somewhat different. The EBA exercise contained the seeds of a future breakthrough. Broadcasting the problems in Europe's banking system was always going to be difficult and dangerous. It risked being criticised as inadequate. But the alternative of doing it behind closed doors, or not doing it at all, as some EBA members would have preferred, would have been worse. By the middle of 2010, a half-good, completely public test was better than no test at all. It reminded everyone there were problems to be resolved. So although judged a failure, the EBA test was actually a step towards a solution.

By the time the EBA published its results in July 2010, it was more or less three years since the onset of the global financial crisis. Although progress had been made globally, the euro area had yet to make those decisions on loss-sharing, central bank funding and monetary expansion necessary to fix the banks and restart economic growth. Most of these things happened, but not for another two years. To paraphrase Vladimir Lenin, in 2010 things needed to get worse before they could get better.

And they did get worse. Fortunately, officials at the International Monetary Fund (IMF) in Washington D.C. were watching events in Europe closely. It issued its own statement in response to the announcement of the EBA results. Although the IMF welcomed the exercise, it added that more needed to be done 'in light of the current turmoil'. These were strong words. They implied that the IMF was finding Europe's attempts to manage its crisis unconvincing.

As we were to discover in a matter of months, this is exactly what Ashoka Mody, one of the IMF's most astute observers of the currency union, was thinking at the time. Fortunately for Ireland and Europe, he was about to get his chance to make a difference.

Lesson #5: Talk about the real issues.

Humanity's relationship with truth has always been a central preoccupation of religion, philosophy, the arts and science, literature and drama. Stories of characters wrestling with truth are found in the major religious texts, great works of literature and plays. They are deeply woven into our culture. We sometimes refer to a person expressing a contrary perspective as a 'voice in the wilderness' or 'an Old Testament prophet'. (It is not usually meant as a compliment.) And if Shakespeare were alive today, and writing *King Lear*, he would have to grant the dissenting Cordelia whistleblower protections. To depart from conventional wisdom has always been, and remains, a hazardous occupation, as we saw in China when COVID-19 first emerged.

These issues are, of course, buried deep in the human psyche. We all have at least one memory of an awkward silence prompted by a truthful observation or comment. We can all recall those moments when the atmosphere in a room changed, when the needle of the emotional barometer moved suddenly. A family Christmas meal where someone has said something. A classroom encounter between a teacher and a bolshie pupil. A meeting at work where the mood shifted dramatically because of something someone has said. These moments can be very revealing. The common thread is that someone will have spoken the truth, or at least articulated something which others may be thinking but dare not say.

A crisis has the same effect. It changes how we see the world, upends our existing narratives. It takes our settled assumptions by the neck, shakes them about and changes the human story. The resulting collision between what we believed, and what is actually true, can be liberating as it allows new narratives to emerge. History is littered with examples of crises having reset the political and social order.

During the global financial crisis, Ireland moved from telling one story about itself to a very different one. This was not a conscious or planned process. All of a sudden, ideas given short shrift in the preceding decade gained a fresh legitimacy. Ireland's awkward silence had been its property boom. When Professor Morgan Kelly, the University College Dublin economist, started to question the sustainability of Ireland's economic model in the mid-2000s, he was ridiculed. When the economy went into freefall, he not only ceased to be a pariah, he became one of the most influential voices in Irish public life.

The business of talking about things no one wants to talk about is integral to crisis prevention and management. We made progress in 2010 and 2011 because we allowed ourselves to talk about those things which were uncomfortable. It is true that we had no choice, but a new narrative had to be created. And that was the opportunity.

During that process I came to recognise that as soon as no one wanted to talk about something, we were probably talking about the right issue. Not all of the time. And not all of the discussions were beneficial. But the avoidance of conflict or truth telling is a luxury we always pay for later. It is better to talk about the things no one wants to talk about before they become the only things they want to talk about.

❇   ❇   ❇

One striking feature of the response to the COVID-19 pandemic was the very public discussion of difficult issues. The likely consequences of the virus for mortality rates. The consequences for healthcare systems if social distancing measures were not observed. The costs to the economy of lifestyle restrictions. This affirmed the maxim that we find it easier to talk about difficult issues when things are difficult. The question which will detain many people in the coming years is whether we were too late in having these conversations.

There is, of course, a limit to the time which can be spent having difficult conversations. In a crisis, time is at a premium. Discussions have to conclude and decisions have to be made. It is neither practical nor desirable to go over the same ground repeatedly. But it is also possible to shut down conversations too soon, to close off potentially fruitful avenues of enquiry. Sometimes this happens because there is not enough time. At other times it is because someone is trying to avoid having a difficult conversation. If this happens, it is reasonable to ask them why, as it is fair to ask them what story it is they wish to tell.

We typically fear these confrontations because of the emotions they trigger, not the subject matter. But as the former hostage negotiator, and business school professor, George Kohlrieser, puts it in his book, *Hostage at the Table*, 'Leaders must understand that conflict can be a major source of creativity and a potential for innovations'. Kohlrieser goes on to explain how conflict can occur constructively. It is sobering to read his advice after having watched world leaders double down on hostile rhetoric during the pandemic. The ability to discuss the issues which matter, to engage with reality, has made human progress possible. The opposite tendency, where discussion is prevented and enquiry blocked, stunts our development. It also makes crises more likely, harder to resolve and influences how long the effects endure. On this seemingly simple point about communication does it seem that much of our fate will turn in the 2020s.

Before COVID-19, the world was struggling to have a conversation about the climate crisis. Will the pandemic change how we approach this issue? As with our response to the outbreak, this is one of the tests ahead of us. We will learn what, if anything, we have learned from this crisis in how we talk about future pandemics, the climate, human development and other issues. If no one wishes to talk about them, or at least is unable to do so in a meaningful, constructive way, future generations will be right to blame us for failing to explore those questions on which human history turns.

Some lessons for leaders in a crisis:

1. **Passive leaders allow problems to fester.** If an issue is so contentious it is commonly thought impossible to be discussed openly, it probably needs to be discussed. One consequence of not doing so is that a problem will only grow and, in all likelihood, become harder to solve. The consequence for a leader is that they will look increasingly weak the longer something is left to fester. This will undermine their credibility and authority. In peacetime, the reckoning for this passivity can take years. In a crisis, the ineffectual leader will have to confront the consequences of inaction almost immediately.

2. **Shape the galvanising narrative.** A crisis provides an opportunity to tackle taboos head on, to debate the issues which really matter. But the bigger prize is to introduce a new narrative, to describe a new reality which will

galvanise a team, overcome long standing obstacles and deliver lasting change.

3. **Decide what needs to be decided.** One of the hardest tasks for any leader is to strike a balance between discussing options and making decisions. A crisis only makes this task more acute. The leader's task is to define what is so important it cannot be left unexamined. At the same time, they must decide what needs to be decided so there is adequate time to debate the big issues.

6.

Eastern Front

Sometimes there is not a cloud above the Irish Sea. On these rare days the views across Ireland, Scotland and Wales are magnificent. If the flight passes the Isle of Man, it is possible to take in its rolling landscape. Until 2010, that is all I had seen of the island. On this occasion I was headed to Douglas proper on a rescue mission, and across the Isle from me sat Dwayne Price, my fellow envoy. We were hunched in the cramped aircraft's small seats as it bounced its way from Dublin. Our objective was to save the Irish banking system.

The Troika's role in Ireland is well-known. Its support enabled Ireland to turn the tide. Less well known is the story of Ireland's relationship with the UK during this period. It was an extraordinary time in Anglo-Irish relations, culminating in Queen Elizabeth's weeklong visit in 2011. Even those with only a vague understanding of Britain's role in Irish history (and vice versa) appreciated its significance. Not only did it have incredible symbolic value. There was a genuine attempt, made on both sides, to reconcile historical differences. This mirrored the constructive and warm relationships between British and Irish officials who worked together to address the effects of the global financial crisis.

But it was not always plain sailing. Anglo-Irish ties were tested during this period. And we knew they were about to be tested again as we looked for a taxi at Douglas airport. We were headed to the island's regulator, the Financial Supervision Commission (FSC).

As a regular user of taxis in Dublin, I was expecting the driver to provide the sort of in-depth analysis about local conditions common to journeys in Dublin. We were disappointed. The only thing more hostile than the weather was the driver's mood. Dwayne and I looked at one another. If his reaction to our simple request was a portent of things to come, it was troubling.

The trip was Matthew Elderfield's fault, in a roundabout way. The FSC had written to him about the Irish banks operating on the island. Some years before, AIB, Anglo Irish Bank and Bank of Ireland had established branches in Douglas. They had done so to raise deposits. Understandably, the FSC wanted to know what actions the Irish authorities were taking to protect depositors.

As a source of funds, the Isle of Man had not been particularly significant to the banks before the crisis. Now, with funding scarce, these deposits counted. But this is not why we made the journey. The big risk was that it might become known that another jurisdiction had restricted Ireland's banks. The billions the banks had raised in Douglas mattered, but being able to operate in Douglas mattered more. This left us with no choice but to meet the Authority face-to-face.

In the days before the trip, I reflected on the approach we might take to the meeting. There was no question that trust in Ireland was at rock bottom. It was fair to assume it would be a difficult conversation. If the FSC had made up its mind beforehand, and wanted to prevent the banks accepting more deposits, I calculated the most we could hope to achieve would be to stall any intervention. We could not offer any meaningful assurances as the Irish government had already played its ace in the form of the guarantee. This was the nub of the issue. The question the FSC would be asking itself is whether the guarantee had any value. But how far would the Isle of Man be willing to go to find out?

While other regulators had asked pointed questions about the health of the Irish banks, none had openly challenged the value of the guarantee. Even if they did doubt its ultimate worth, it was not the done thing for one EU member state to question the solvency of another. Although it was not clear from the Isle of Man's request exactly what it did want, we assumed it wanted to show it was doing something. So while its letter was irksome, we saw no merit in deflecting the Isle of Man's enquiry. A dismissive or high-handed response would do more harm than good. And if the FSC was seriously considering restrictions on Irish banks, we needed to find this out sooner rather than later.

Not that this was a one-sided issue. The stakes were high for the Isle of Man. The Irish banks had gathered meaningful deposits in the local market, with the FSC's approval. If the worst happened, and one or more of the Irish banks did not repay depositors, the costs might fall on the island's government. Not only would this be expensive, it would be damaging to the Isle of Man's reputation. In the competitive world of offshore financial centres, such a setback would hurt. Financial services contributed disproportionately to the island's economy. The FSC had every right to understand what was happening in Dublin. And it had every reason to be *seen* to do so.

Dwayne and I were intent on being open-minded and receptive, fully expecting this to be reciprocated. We were therefore disconcerted when we arrived at the FSC's office in Douglas. The welcome was cool. After a long wait in reception, we were taken to a meeting room. My heart sank when the chairman introduced us: 'Mr McMahon and Mr Price, from the Central Bank of Ireland.' Her tone was stiff and formal. Perhaps a Manx trait, I told myself, reflecting on the taxi journey.

The FSC's board members were seated around a horseshoe shaped table. It was not unlike a parliamentary committee, but I had not prepared myself for a Manx Star Chamber. I was momentarily disconcerted. The usual pre-meeting pleasantries were also omitted. There was no opportunity to shake hands with FSC board members, no chance for small talk or to build rapport. Instead, we were asked to sit in front of the group.

The chairman explained our reasons for being there. She gave the FSC's assessment of the Irish banks. Had I closed my eyes, I might have opened them on a judge reciting a list of charges. We had made the journey confident that some straight answers, and a little charm, might be enough to address the FSC's concerns. After five minutes, I was starting to wonder whether we would soon be returning to Dublin to explain why the Irish banks were being ejected from the Isle of Man. This would not have been a good outcome.

It took some time, but eventually a less adversarial tone developed. The other FSC board members appeared more relaxed than the chairman. As they asked their questions, the mood in the room shifted. Despite my earlier fears, it seemed that the FSC had not pre-judged the discussion after all. There was a genuine interest in the situation in Ireland. I sensed some empathy. We shared information which it would have been hard to do in writing. Dwayne's confident description of the banks suggested we understood the issues and had a plan (of sorts). We were evidently making some headway.

And so it proved. We were called back into the room and thanked for our time and candour. Perhaps the chairman and chief executive had wanted this result. If so, they had managed the process well. They knew we could say nothing about the value of the government guarantee. They knew there would be only so much we could say about the banks. We appeared to have addressed whatever concerns had motivated the FSC to write in the first place. Doubtless there is a record of the meeting in Douglas which says as much.

This meeting spoke to some larger truths about the changing role and perception of the guarantee as the crisis developed. At the time it was put in place, the economist and *Financial Times* contributor, Willem Buiter, attacked it as a beggar-thy-neighbour policy. Some questioned its legality. The European Commission spent a lot of time working out whether or not it was acceptable under EU law. By 2010, however, the value of the guarantee was openly being questioned within and outside Ireland. Our trip to Douglas confirmed it was, by then, of more symbolic than practical value. But even as a symbol of the government's commitment, it had some worth. I was never asked whether the Irish government was committed to its banks. This is not an unimportant fact. Even as its practical worth diminished, it still engendered some confidence.

Where it threatened to become a problem was between Dublin and London. The UK government did not hide its displeasure when it learned about the guarantee. The chancellor at the time, Alistair Darling, reacted furiously. He saw it as damaging to British banks. On a visit to Dublin in 2011 to promote his memoir of the crisis, *Back from the Brink*, he relived the moment he found out. It was obviously still something which needled him. In my own discussions with UK officials, it remained a talking point. It did not do any permanent damage, but it had temporarily impaired trust.

But it was one of only a few wrinkles in a largely otherwise constructive relationship in the crisis years. After all, the UK government had its own reasons for wanting Ireland to achieve a soft landing. This was a peculiar time for me. I had the same accent as the officials I would meet from Treasury and Bank of England. Like them, I was born and raised in Britain. But for some twists and turns in my own career, I could have been sitting on the other side of the table. Whether in these bilateral forums, or at the EBA table or elsewhere, I was incredibly proud to represent Ireland. But I was alive to the irony of my situation when dealing with my British counterparts.

I was especially conscious of my hybrid status when we negotiated the bilateral loan between the UK and Irish governments. Following the completion of the March 2011 stress test, the euro area had agreed a support package for Ireland. The bilateral loan sat alongside the euro area facility. It was kept deliberately separate as the UK government had made it very clear it did not want to expose UK taxpayers to the euro area crisis. George Osborne, the chancellor, also knew it would have been politically toxic within the governing Conservative Party to have done so. But of all the member states of the EU, the UK had the greatest interest in seeing Ireland bounce back. It therefore wanted to find a way to support Ireland. The most senior officials on both sides, Kevin Cardiff and his opposite number at the Treasury, Nick Macpherson, therefore began the process to agree a loan.

The end result was a simple and fair agreement which helped the Irish State's overall debt burden. It said something for the spirit of the times that even the most Anglophobic commentators struggled to present it as a national humiliation. One writer tried to evoke memories of British army recruitment in Ireland, making a reference to 'the taking of the Queen's shilling'. But this was wide of the mark, not least because it ignored the fact that the terms were at least as favourable as Ireland's other EU partners were offering. Most people saw the loan, correctly in my view, as the practical expression of an effective relationship.

I was part of the Irish team which negotiated the loan. I did not see any evidence of inferiority on one side or superiority on the other. The Department of Finance's William Beausang, a thoughtful man with a strong sense of history, made a couple of light-hearted references to previous Anglo-Irish negotiations. This told its own story. Past difficulties could, by 2011, be referenced in this manner. The sessions were certainly cordial and professional; there was mutual respect, and there was a shared desire to address a common problem.

But there were missteps in this relationship. The first one I witnessed followed the decision to place Quinn Insurance into administration. Although Quinn did most of its business in the Republic of Ireland, it had established a branch in the UK. It did this under EU rules designed to encourage cross-border competition. Even before it entered administration,

UK regulators had developed some concerns about Quinn Insurance. But it was only a small operation and, as a branch, it was the Central Bank's responsibility.

In the context of the Quinn Group, the UK business was inconsequential. We nonetheless kept our UK counterparts informed of developments, before and after Quinn entered administration, sharing more information than EU rules required. This ought to have been more than sufficient. But in what proved to be a revealing series of interactions, an official at the FCA started to make additional demands of the Central Bank. He also raised the prospect of unilateral action against Quinn Insurance in the UK. This set teeth on edge in Dublin, including my own.

At the time, I regarded the UK official's reaction as disproportionate. Even if we allowed for his quirks (with which Matthew and I were familiar), his demands provided an insight into the UK regulatory mindset. UK regulators had received their own share of criticism for their handling of the crisis. Doubtless no one in London wanted to be caught out by another problem originating across the Irish Sea. Some hair-trigger behaviour in London was explicable.

But we found it hard to accept the none too subtle disregard for EU law. We were responsible for the branch in every respect, save for its adherence to local rules on how it conducted business. But the issue was not how Quinn was conducting business. The issue was its solvency. The correct response was for the UK to defer to Ireland, and not simply because this is what EU law said. In a situation where the solvency of a business is at risk, cooperation between regulators is incredibly important. A clumsy intervention can trigger the event one is seeking to prevent. We were working hard to preserve jobs and value at Quinn. If the UK had placed restrictions on the UK business, this would have worked against these efforts. Sadly, the UK official did not greatly trouble himself to understand why the situation was so delicate.

We were eventually able to reach an agreement on the UK branch which enabled the UK official to stand down. But it had been an unnecessary distraction at a time when we needed to concentrate our limited firepower on the main issues at the parent company in Ireland. Not only had London ignored EU protocols, it had done so in a high-handed and officious manner. This was hardly the stuff of Anglo-Irish solidarity. And it left a bad taste in Irish mouths. They resented the UK swerving out of its regulatory lane. One senior Irish official wondered whether we ought to ignore the FCA's demands. I saw his point. But fighting fire with fire would have created more problems.

While this was a troublesome episode, it was not of great importance. But it was a reminder that London was nervous about Irish financial institutions operating in the UK. In particular, it was nervous about the Irish banks.

Like Quinn Insurance, Irish banks had taken advantage of EU rules to establish branches in the UK. The branch model was attractive as it did not require the overheads of a subsidiary. Nor did a branch require its own capital. Branches also received less attention from local regulators as most of the risks sat with the country of origin. But as the crisis developed, host regulators across Europe became increasingly uncomfortable with this model, despite the fact that banks were legally entitled to operate as branches. The UK in particular started to take a tougher line. It worried that deposits raised in the UK, but not receiving the protection of the UK's own deposit insurance scheme, were more at risk. The Irish banks were not the only ones under the spotlight, but they were a major source of concern for UK officials.

Bank of Ireland's UK branch was near the top-of-the-worry list. It raised deposits through the Post Office. It is hard to imagine a more iconic and politically sensitive distribution channel. For as long as Bank of Ireland retained a branch structure, the Irish rather than UK deposit insurance scheme protected savers. This had attracted little interest from UK regulators before the crisis. But as pressure built on the Irish banks, so concern grew among UK politicians and officials about the security of UK depositors. The demographic of Post Office customers only heightened this anxiety. Equally, since the Post Office was associated in the popular imagination with the Royal Mail, and therefore the government itself, ministers worried this might lead savers to assume the UK government backed their deposits. In one account, Peter Mandelson, at that time the UK's Business Secretary, is said to have reacted in horror when told that Post Office savers were actually Bank of Ireland depositors. Pressure therefore built on UK regulators to find a way to protect savers and the UK taxpayer.

Their solution was to make Bank of Ireland create a separately capitalised subsidiary in the UK. This brought Sterling deposits within the scope of the UK's compensation scheme. It gave the UK regulator greater control and, correspondingly, reduced the Central Bank's role in oversight of the UK entity.

For the bank, there were three further consequences. Capital, which had always been transferable within the group, could no longer move freely between its Irish and UK entities, leaving some of its capital trapped in the UK. It also meant its

UK management were answerable to UK regulations and had to follow UK rules. This reduced the influence of the group's management, including its CEO, Richie Boucher. Finally, and most ominously, the new UK subsidiary fell within the scope of Britain's newly created Special Resolution Regime.

The powers available under this regime were extensive. It was one of Gordon Brown's flagship reforms following the collapse of Northern Rock. The new regime allowed the UK authorities to take control of a failing bank to protect depositors and manage the risk of contagion. From an Irish perspective, the Special Resolution Regime changed the balance of power with UK regulators. Our counterparts in London suddenly had the ability to make life or death decisions about the Irish banks. We could do little if they exercised these new powers.

We therefore needed to do everything to prevent this happening. This meant increasing our efforts to foster confidence and trust among decision makers in London. Although Matthew and I had good networks in Britain, many people had moved jobs during the crisis. There were also new jobs in the two regulators, the Financial Conduct Authority and Prudential Regulatory Authority. The Special Resolution Unit, at the Bank of England, was also one of the crisis creations. It was imperative that we developed a relationship with this team. I therefore travelled to London to meet them. This included the team's then boss at the Bank of England, Andrew Bailey, now Governor of the Bank of England.

The Bank's home on Threadneedle Street has the feel of a public school or Oxbridge college. The pink suited doormen, long echoing corridors and memorials to the fallen of two world wars locate it at the centre of the British establishment.

Its officials, always bright and pleasant, have donnish traits which match their surroundings.

All of these attributes were on full display as I sat down with the Special Resolution Unit. They were terribly polite. They explained how the new regime worked. In a very indirect way, they articulated their concerns about the Irish banks operating in the UK. They did not say they were measuring a body for a funeral, but I sensed this to be exactly what they were doing. As I sat and listened, it did not take me long to conclude we had a potential problem on our hands.

I explained what we were doing to restore the Irish banks to something approaching health. I was deliberately candid. The team listened carefully. They made notes. They asked questions. They knew what I knew: for as long as there were doubts about the health of the Irish State, there would be doubts about the banks. They asked me what I thought would happen to Bank of Ireland's UK subsidiary if there was a run on its Irish parent. It was a fair but, I told myself, leading question. Although the creation of the UK subsidiary had distanced it from its Irish parent, it would not have insulated it completely. It carried the same name. The British media would have linked it to Ireland and not given too much credit to the bank's different legal status in the UK. I could understand why the Special Resolution Unit would want its own contingency plan for the UK bank.

Not that they hid their concerns. They were clearly sympathetic to the problems we faced, but they had little appetite for another disorderly bank failure. This would impact confidence in UK banks. There would be a cost to the UK deposit insurance scheme. The regulator itself would come under the spotlight. The media and politicians would ask why it had been given new powers if it was not going to use them. We had already concluded the new regime was a threat to Irish banks and, by extension, our own work. The meeting confirmed we were right to be concerned.

But it also confirmed that they wanted to work with us rather than against us. The team had no appetite to make things more difficult for their Irish colleagues. This was a very different experience from Quinn Insurance, in tone and substance. There were no threats. There was no attempt to force Ireland down a path it did not wish to take. In a very calm and deliberate way, they described how they saw the situation, and what might cause them to intervene. But they also made it clear they would work with the Irish authorities. This was reassuring as we could not allow an already difficult situation becoming unmanageable.

The UK did not, in the end, take a tougher line. The UK's broader strategic interest in Ireland was always likely to act as a brake on any hasty or heavy-handed interventions. At working level, UK officials were sensitive to the challenges facing Ireland. They had, after all, faced their own banking problems. But any complacency on our side would have been dangerous. While the UK authorities found a way to bridge their demands and our needs, it was our job to remind them of the consequences of any actions against Irish banks.

These interactions said much about the damage the crisis had done to confidence in Ireland. It also said much about the changing dynamics of regulation and regulatory cooperation, especially in the EU. There had always been strong arguments for regulators to work together to supervise the global financial system. Although the financial crisis crossed borders, governments and regulators had retreated, preferring nation-state solutions to what were increasingly presented as nation-state problems. Ireland was particularly exposed to these developments as it needed help from other governments and regulators. It therefore said much for Anglo-Irish cooperation that some very challenging issues were addressed constructively during this period.

To the credit of politicians and officials on both sides of the Irish Sea, substance-over-form decisions were taken when major issues presented themselves, such as the guarantee, the treatment of the Irish banks in the UK, the treatment of British banks in Ireland, and the bilateral loan. There were niggles, but these proved to be of no lasting consequence. If anything, the UK and Ireland found ways of working together which were more effective than those between Ireland and its euro area partners. While there was some measure of self-interest for both countries, it also reflected a level of sympathy in London which was not always evident in Berlin, Paris or Frankfurt.

Lesson #6: Don't just understand the numbers, understand their meaning.

I have worked in organisations where calculations were regularly performed in billions of pounds, euros or dollars. The clients of one of these organisations owned assets worth billions of pounds. Another had made loans worth billions of euros. But I never saw any actual money. I never saw hundreds of lorries transporting billions in notes and coins. I saw figures on pieces of paper and numbers on screens. But like everyone else, I had to trust that the money existed, even if no one could say exactly where it was to be found.

This is the nature of money in the modern economy: numbers on screens. So why the obsession with something we so rarely see? And why, when we hold paper and metal in our hands, or stare at our bank balance on our phone, do we invest these symbols with meaning?

I used to think that everyone took the pieces of paper and screens so seriously because the numbers were so big. There was evidently much at stake, much to be gained, much to be lost. The earnest demeanour of accountants I met early in my career reinforced this perception. They discussed money as if it were real, talked about its importance to decisions, and sometimes behaved as if it were the only factor to be considered when making choices. The further I penetrated this elaborate ecosystem, the more detached I became from what I knew to be true about money: that it is not real.

The global financial crisis reminded everyone of the troubling truth that money relies on trust. The queues which formed outside Northern Rock branches in 2007 were a sharp reminder of the fragile nature of this trust. They were also a reminder that many cling to an idea that money is only tangible in its every day, exchangeable form: physical cash. That same every day form I never saw, despite being surrounded by billions of the stuff, apparently.

The financial crisis was not only a crisis involving money as an object. It was also a struggle about the meaning of money. It was blindingly obvious that money mattered in a very practical sense as it was the measure of value, the yardstick of the financial system's health. But the crisis also led many to question whether they could trust the idea of money. To question not whether something was worth x or y, but whether the measure of x or y was itself to be trusted.

This was a subtle, largely unconscious, and therefore psychologically complex reaction. Before the crisis, we held an idea about money in our minds and invested it with symbolic value. As the crisis dragged on, our confidence in the symbol wavered. Our belief in the idea of money was, in other words, weakened.

Or at least one aspect of this belief was under threat. One of the functions of money is to serve as a store of value. It is a means of counting something someone owns. A way of valuing, in technical jargon, a right to property. But what happens when this accounting measure is no longer reliable? What if it cannot be trusted? What would this mean for ownership rights?

The crisis brought these questions to the fore. It exposed the fact that the financial system, looked at in one way, is no more than a collection of ownership rights, where the value of these rights is expressed in monetary terms. A bank deposit creates a right to receive income in the form of interest. A share in a company creates a right to vote (and possibly receive income in the form of a dividend payment). These rights are valuable. But they are also largely intangible. As Northern Rock's customers demonstrated, physical cash was psychologically more valuable to them than a legal right to a deposit.

The crisis also reminded us that these rights, and how they were valued, also, like money, depend on trust. People not only feared they would lose value when banks failed and markets tumbled. They feared that their rights to ownership would become worthless, either because there was simply nothing of value, or because the valuation basis changed. This is why the future of the euro became such a preoccupation for markets in 2010. People could see that one currency, with a lower value, might replace another, with a higher value.

This was a very real problem for Ireland since external investors faced a potential double-hit to value. A bank loan which might never be repaid, valued in a currency which might no longer exist, is not an attractive asset. It is hardly surprising this dented confidence in the financial system and bred uncertainty. There was, to put it differently, little psychological safety if the rules underpinning the system of trust might dissolve overnight.

Looked at through the lens of economic theory, these reactions were irrational. The economic critique of the boom was that people were too optimistic about the future. The same critique of the crisis was that they were too pessimistic. Since it is economists who, for the most part, write about financial crises, this is how we tend to think about them. But it is not, in my view, a sufficiently broad frame of reference. When trying to interpret, or for that matter manage, a crisis, we have to look beyond economics. If we limit ourselves to describing a crisis as an irrational deviation from a rational norm, all we are doing is using one set of ideas to describe another. As the psychiatrist, Iain McGilchrist, said in *The Master and His Emissary: The Divided Brain and the Making of the Western World*, 'The model we choose to use to understand something determines what we find'.

A crisis not only exposes the limits to the explanatory power of economics and finance, it reminds us of the importance of human psychology. The financial system relies on trust, and trust is exclusively the currency of the human mind. We therefore need a highly plausible set of ideas to sustain our trust in this system. But this is only the starting point. Our lived experience, the reality we encounter, must accord to these ideas. If it does not, trust will evaporate. We are programmed to react to uncertainty, to spot gaps between what we observe and what we feel, between what someone says and what they do. We are constantly questioning our own beliefs, consciously and unconsciously. We are continually refreshing our understanding of the world. Our ideas about finance, and the stories we tell ourselves about money, are therefore incredibly important. And during the global financial crisis we started to question them.

But when it comes to money and finance, we seem to believe that different rules apply, that stories are trivial. That finance is properly the domain of the rational human being, only to be understood through charts and figures, accountants and actuaries, plausible men in suits. But finance and economics are not reality, any more than a map is the territory or a menu is the meal.

Why has this happened? Why have we adopted near religious belief in economics as an explanatory tool? We are conditioned from an early age to believe that mathematics provides an unimpeachable description of reality. But while finance makes use of mathematics, it is not a branch of mathematics. The confusion is understandable, but it is mistaken.

As is our habit of placing too much weight on numerical calculations which purport to describe reality. In both crises, we leaned on models which were wrong. Before the global financial crisis, we relied on models designed to estimate risk. During the pandemic, we used models built to understand virus transmission. The flaws in these pandemic models are likely to be exposed in the coming years, as the flaws in the banks' models were laid bare after 2008. But our big mistake, in both crises, was to hope that the abstractions these models produced might deliver something approaching predictive certainty.

Why do we keep making this mistake? Perhaps if astrologers or horse racing tipsters had doctorates in mathematics or astrophysics, we would attach more weight to their predictions. However, we seem to be drawn towards the idea that because someone is adept at constructing an elaborate mathematical model, they can somehow see the future. But this is not their fault. It is ours for indulging an innate desire for greater certainty in an uncertain world.

But if we are guilty of attaching too much meaning to certain numbers, there is no exit from a crisis unless the numbers which matter to its resolution are identified. In the global financial crisis, the key number was the amount of new capital the banking system required. In the early phases of the pandemic, the key number was the rate of new infections. In both crises, officials needed to know these numbers in order to address the root causes. But they soon realised that these numbers had acquired symbolic significance in the public's imagination. This not only made them important as practical measures to be used in policy formulation, they were psychologically significant too. The average citizen may not have understood the first thing about bank capital or infection rates, but they could grasp what a jump or drop in those figures signified. And their reaction to an increase or decrease would influence that all-important feeling of confidence essential to crisis management.

Put differently, the numbers mattered in their own right, but their meaning mattered more.

❆   ❆   ❆

On 22 March 2020, Donald Trump tweeted that the lockdown cure could not be worse than the COVID-19 disease. This prompted predictable reactions from the right and left in American politics. Few paused to ask how such a deceptively simple trade-off might be evaluated. The process of defining the measures, let alone structuring an answer, would be fiendishly difficult, not least because of the need to weigh ethical and moral issues. Not that this stopped the President. As his scientific advisors attempted to shape policy based on scientific measures, Trump looked at the economic and stock market data. He had the final say on which numbers counted, even if it was not clear they were the ones which mattered.

From its outset, the pandemic triggered a desperate struggle by governments globally to work out which numbers mattered to policy decisions, and for those which did, what they meant. This had a strange parallel in the experience of those working to save lives in emergency rooms. As medical professionals battled to understand how this new virus was impacting patients, they were confronted with countless data points. Which measures of a patient's health mattered? Could unfamiliar data be relied upon to determine interventions? Which medicines worked? As the reliability of medical data improved, so the quality of treatment got better. As the meaning of different symptoms were better understood, and the relationship between the virus and other medical conditions grasped, so the medical response improved. But this was only achieved through trial and error.

As the outbreak developed, we started to understand the true meaning of the reported numbers. Contrary to early assessments, it became clear this was not just another influenza-type virus. It was far more dangerous to the old than the young. We also began to comprehend how it spread, and therefore why adequate personal protective equipment (PPE) in hospitals and care homes was important to deter its transmission. Much of this could only be learned through experience, so officials were, for a time, left to fly blind. They may have had the numbers, but they could not be sure what they meant.

In an albeit very different context, this reflected the experience in the early stages of the global financial crisis. It is no accident that the metaphors of disease and contagion are used to describe financial crises. From 2007, officials talked in these terms. They were desperate to know which financial institutions were most vulnerable, who was carrying toxic portfolios. And in a striking parallel with the pandemic, officials had to test the system to find out who was infected. The stress tests of the global financial crisis were the swabs of the COVID-19 pandemic.

In both crises, testing occurred in conditions of heightened uncertainty, not least because officials were obliged to measure a moving target. The efficacy of the available tests was also open to question. And in both 2008 and 2020, test results came back before much could be done with the results. Only in 2011, after a number of attempts, did Ireland complete a stress test which definitively answered the questions being asked about its banks. Only many months into the pandemic did many European countries get their act together on testing (lagging the success of many better prepared Asian nations). Not only did this make it much harder to manage both crises. It made it harder to show the problem was being managed and, therefore, to build confidence.

During the COVID-19 pandemic it certainly took governments a while to grasp this point. The early official messages talked about infection rates, mortality rates and at-risk cohorts within populations. We were presented with graphs and tables showing the likely spread of COVID-19. The proposed remedies were explained in calm, rational terms. It might as well have been a presentation about inflation and interest rates. While it doubtless made perfect sense for policymakers to think in this way, it did little to foster emotional engagement. It was too abstract. By contrast, the simple and direct 'Stay at Home, Save Lives' message in the UK resonated immediately. People wanted to save lives. They were not motivated to move a line on a chart, nor driven to flatten a curve. Yet this was the outcome: the lines moved, the curve flattened. Why? Because people understood the consequences of the numbers, not the actual numbers. They understood the meaning, even if they did not comprehend the final detail of the calculations.

Throughout the pandemic a tug-of-war occurred between those who grasped this point, and could tell a story, and those who were seemingly trapped within the numbers. But this is true of all crises, whether at the level of a company, a sector of an economy or an entire nation. Those comfortable to talk in personal terms, comfortable to tell empathetic yet honest stories, are always the more effective communicators. Those who, in other words, make the numbers serve a greater narrative, rather than let the numbers decide the story.

We will learn much in the coming years about what did and did not work in official communications during the pandemic. We will better understand what motivated citizens to stick to rules which, ordinarily, might have led to civil unrest. And in a few years' time, it is unlikely we will remember how many people died, but we will be able to recall the stories and faces of those lost to the virus, as we will the stories of those who were on the frontline. We will, in other words, understand the meaning of numbers we will have long forgotten.

Some lessons for leaders in a crisis:

1. **Financial problems can be like Russian dolls**. A financial crisis presents complex problems which often need to be unravelled before they can be understood. Where a reported number is an aggregate of other figures, or is based on assumptions, there will be a need to understand the basis of the calculation, as well as the significance (or otherwise) of its constituent parts. This is time well spent when managing an input to a major decision, not least because the smallest doll in the set may be the most significant to the overall calculation.

2. **Make sure you have enough right-brain people.** Since finance tends to be dominated by analytical, left-brain types, such as accountants and actuaries, there can be a lack of balance around a leader. Analytical people are important in a crisis. But equally important are people who understand human behaviour, how people receive and process information and who themselves can craft

a story. It is the leader's responsibility to make sure they have these people on their team.

3. **Numbers do not make sense without a story.** Unless we understand the thing to which it relates, we will not understand the number or why it matters. We also need to understand how it relates to other numbers. Unless we understand these relationships, we will be unable to grasp what story the numbers are telling us. The leader needs to ensure the story is clearly told.

7.

Waiting for Ashoka

Even during the darkest days of Dublin's crisis, the Rock Road, one of the city's main north-south routes, was busy with German-built cars. I cycled this route regularly, weaving between these prestige marques, many purchased during the boom years. On days when I was due to meet the ECB, I counted the cars I knew had been built in Stuttgart, Munich, Ingolstadt, Rastatt, Wolfsburg and other centres of automotive production in Germany. There were hundreds, a point I would mischievously make to the ECB. Although not many of them had been bought recently, here, on one of Dublin's busiest roads, was the evidence for why austerity in one part of the euro area was bad for another.

The Rock Road started and finished in Dublin. The route out of the crisis ran through Frankfurt and Berlin. As the euro area's largest and most important member, many looked to Germany for answers to the crisis. Yet despite being the big winner from the euro, it seemed outwardly reluctant to keep the project going. The benefits to Germany were unarguable. Its export-led economy depended on trade. Its exports could be priced in Euros, far below the likely price in Deutschmarks. As a consequence, the German economy had expanded consistently. But just as Germany reached the summit of its economic and political power, the foundations supporting its ascent were crumbling.

Why did Germany not act more decisively to end the euro area crisis? This will be a debating point for years to come. Had Ireland's banking crisis been the only problem, perhaps Germany might have shown less hesitation. It would have been a much smaller problem for a start. But the euro area's difficulties did not begin and end in Dublin. Nor did anyone know the extent of the problem for the euro area as a whole. The suspicions of many, including many Germans, was that Berlin could be drawn into supporting much of Southern Europe. This understandably limited Berlin's appetite to intervene. It also increased the attraction of postponing difficult decisions. But the price of political hesitancy in 2010 was a deepening crisis. The euro area's financial system continued to bear the brunt of this uncertainty. The populations of Greece, Ireland and Portugal bore the economic reversals. The net result for Ireland was to make it harder for the banks and public finances to stage any form of recovery.

In the absence of a political silver bullet, the ECB remained the euro area's principal shock absorber. But divided internally, unsure of itself and faced with opponents on the inside, the ECB had few straightforward choices, but it did have choices. It could have chosen a different path. But in the early stages of the global financial crisis, there was a crisis of leadership in Frankfurt. And like any organisation unsure of its preferred direction, it opted to choose no direction in particular.

This became a major problem as the crisis deepened in 2010. What had started as a banking and sovereign debt crisis in some of the smaller euro area countries had become a currency crisis. Not a crisis of value but an existential crisis about the currency union itself. The question, on a number of lips, was whether the euro would survive. I witnessed this first-hand in Dublin. The branch of the giant Dutch bank, Rabobank, started to attract serious inflows of deposits. This was because they enjoyed the protection of the Dutch rather than the Irish government. And the Netherlands was more likely to remain in the currency union.

This story started to gain attention in 2010. This led to articles in serious news outlets about whether a Dutch or German euro might be worth more than a Greek, Irish or Spanish one. Attempts were made to estimate the different values of these notionally national euros. Something un-thinkable a few years earlier was now being openly discussed. And as depositors started to move euros between different countries, a silent, slow bank run had begun. The euro looked like it might unravel.

These developments did not galvanise the ECB. Nor did it show any signs of moderating its stance towards Ireland and the Irish banks. It wanted its money back. Frankfurt's envoy to Ireland (and Greece), Klaus Masuch, acknowledged the strains on the Irish State when he arrived in Dublin in 2010. But he was adamant that the ECB's very large expo-sure to Ireland had to be reduced. Did the Irish banks' well publicised difficulties exacerbate his concerns? He certainly seemed eager to be repaid sooner rather than later. We ex-plained at some length that rapid deleveraging would make the problem worse rather than better.

So began a game of cat and mouse which lasted until July 2011. But the odds were not wholly in the cat's favour. The Irish mouse, although ailing, had swallowed just enough poison to be a danger to the ECB. Ireland had more than enough debt with the ECB to give it leverage. But there was little appetite among Irish officials to establish how much leverage. This was, in hindsight, an error. The ECB was evidently a nervous creditor. The unconvincing way in which it toyed with the Irish mouse confirmed this impression. Behind the bluster was a hint it might give ground in a negotiation. Even so, there was no desire in Dublin to take on the ECB publicly.

The Irish media was less shy. It understood the dynamics of Ireland's debt position. It gave a platform to writers who advocated a full or partial default on bank debt. Professor Morgan Kelly of University College Dublin was the most outspoken. In November 2010, he put his boot into the government and Central Bank, claiming the crisis had deprived the country of its sovereignty. While this was not too far wide of the mark, his prediction of social conflict, 'on the scale of the Land War', seemed overdone. Yet there were serious problems in the mortgage market, and the government debt position was getting worse by the day. Kelly may have overstated the problems, and their possible consequences, but in mid-November 2010, even his crude glancing blow was enough to disorientate officials already anxious about market sentiment and the mood in the country.

The psychology of that moment mattered more than any of us realised at the time. A sort of siege mentality had set in. There was a feeling among officials they were losing the public relations battle. There was an unspoken fear that perhaps Kelly was right and the officials wrong. That Ireland should repudiate the guarantee. That it should turn Ireland's toxic banks into a strength, use the ECB's weight against it, and not tamely accept Frankfurt's instructions on when and how it would be repaid.

This was the key issue: how and when Frankfurt would get its money back. Both parties needed to come to an agreement. But they also needed to decide how aggressive, or otherwise, they would be in pursuing them. Would Ireland adopt a confrontational posture as Greece had done? Or would it be more accommodating? Would the ECB insist on rapid deleveraging? Would it force Ireland to rely more on ELA? All of these questions were yet to be decided.

But this was a very strange state of affairs. Ireland was, in effect, in an argument with its own central bank. And this was not the sort of policy argument which occurs as a matter of course between governments and central banks. This was a full blown encounter about the very survival of a banking system. A confrontation about the burden Irish taxpayers should have to carry to satisfy the requirements of an unelected institution outside democratic accountability. There were many in Ireland who thought the ECB was being difficult and obstructive. There were a few who thought it was overstepping. To yield to its demands would, in their assessment, be to subordinate Irish democracy to an unelected and unaccountable institution.

So while the arguments of 2010 might have been about money, they were also about how the euro area worked. The rights of nations. The rights of creditors. The ECB's role. Its accountability to a democratically elected government. Burden sharing within a currency union. As we sat in Dublin with the ECB's representatives, these might not have seemed the most urgent issues, but they soon became the most pressing. We needed to secure cheap central bank funding for the Irish banks. It wanted the opposite outcome.

I never saw anything to suggest that my colleagues wanted to play hardball with the ECB. This undoubtedly reflected a view that euro membership limited their freedom of action. But this was not the whole story. There was something else going on. Something less tangible. Something in the psyche of Irish officials which influenced how they thought about Europe. A belief system founded on the idea that Ireland belonged in Europe, that Europe was unquestionably good for Ireland, that the European project had delivered prosperity and a more liberal and tolerant social order. It should hardly be surprising that its most senior politicians and officials made the same association, and acted accordingly.

There was also a sense among Irish officials that, as a smaller country, Ireland lacked influence in Europe. This was not an unrealistic perspective; the political realities of Europe said as much. But a cool-headed assessment of one's place in the world is one thing. An absence of self-belief is another. And the difference matters in diplomacy as much as it does in life. The sense that it was not 'very Irish' to believe Ireland could (and should) push its own interests had some influence on events in those years.

The crisis had, of course, done little to alter this self-perception. I found this fascinating as an outsider with some experience of Whitehall. Dublin may be only 465 kilometres from London, but the world definitely looks different from the British capital for a British official than it does in Dublin for an Irish official. And this difference is not only explained by the relative size of the two countries. It reflects a divergent state of mind.

Michael Noonan, the Finance Minister, most famously expressed the Irish government's unwillingness to throw its weight around when, in his thick Limerick burr, he said, 'We are not going to burn the bondholders'. He made this statement when many commentators were calling for burden sharing with creditors. The most senior Irish officials, Kevin Cardiff and Patrick Honohan, were also intellectually and temperamentally inclined towards compromise. Both understood and accepted the obligations which came with euro membership, including the need to make sacrifices to contribute to financial stability in the euro area. Furthermore, they both disliked conflict. With Kevin and Patrick in charge, the ECB would never be able to bully Ireland. But neither would it encounter a belligerent opponent determined to frustrate it at every turn.

What puzzled me was why the ECB failed to understand the state of mind of Irish politicians and officials. Ireland did not wish to be a source of instability in the euro area. It wanted to remain in the euro. It was committed to the European project. The ECB not only missed these points, but at times behaved towards Ireland as if it were an opponent. Kevin and Patrick took great care to explain to the ECB that Ireland was committed to repaying eurosystem funding. There was therefore no difference of view about the ultimate objective. Where the two sides differed was about how and when the ECB loans should be repaid. There was talk in the media about an alternative, hardball strategy. But it always remained a fringe position among officials. Quite why the ECB acted as if Ireland was an existential threat therefore remains a puzzle. The Irish chose cooperation. The ECB chose conflict. It was difficult for trust to develop between the ECB and Irish authorities in these conditions, which only made it harder to find a solution.

The nub of the disagreement between Ireland and the ECB was about the scale and pace of bank deleveraging. The ECB wanted Irish banks to sell loans and contract their balance sheets. But deleveraging might well push an already weak economy into a deflationary spiral. It took Japan a decade to escape deflation following its own credit crisis. Unless Ireland could return to growth, more jobs would be lost, incomes would fall further and more homes would be repossessed.

This is always the consequence of deflation. But even when it has been consciously used as a policy tool to reduce inflation, for example in 1980s Britain, there are typically off-setting fiscal measures, as well as a currency which can adjust and therefore take some of the strain. The ECB's plan neither envisaged nor enabled such cushioning measures. Under its formula, Greece, Ireland and Portugal were expected to pay their debts while their economies contracted. In other words, more was requested of less. This was reckless. The damage to the social fabric could have been significant – a point we made repeatedly to the ECB (and anyone else who would listen).

The ECB reasoned that the proceeds from loan sales could be used to repay ECB borrowings. There were numerous problems with this deceptively simple request. For a start, there were few, if any, buyers. Even where a purchaser might be found, deflation meant a buyer would have to be willing to catch a falling knife. There was accordingly little interest in

Irish assets. And since no one knew how much worse things might become, investors decided to wait.

There was another major flaw in the ECB's deleveraging plan. It understood that when banks sell loans at a loss they have to use capital. But the banks had no capital, and their only source of new money was a government fast running out of cash. The best that could be said of the ECB's stance was that it was going to bring everything to a head very quickly, if not in a way which was necessarily going to benefit the ECB.

No one in Dublin was against loan sales in principle. They were against the policy at the wrong point in the economic cycle. But even if the economy had been in better shape, it is doubtful the ECB's objectives could have been met. For a potential buyer to determine value, there has to be a process of price discovery. This depends on there being readily available and, crucially, reliable information. In 2010, there was little confidence about the true worth of banks' loans. The banks had dropped lending standards so far during the crisis that even they did not understand the true picture. This was far from the functioning market ECB orthodoxy required if its policy was to work.

At its headquarters in Washington, DC, 5,439 kilometres away, the IMF watched this standoff develop. Normally in a crisis as severe as the ones in Greece, Ireland and Portugal, the IMF would have long since rolled into town. But it had no mandate to intervene in the euro area, and had not been asked to help. The IMF had therefore limited itself to statements designed to encourage discussion of solutions. But until it was invited to provide assistance, it could do nothing.

This was a source of frustration in Washington. Unlike the ECB, the IMF had deep experience of crisis management. It did not have the ECB's mandate, powers or financial muscle, but as it always worked closely with central banks in crisis-hit countries, this was not, in theory at least, an obstacle to its participation in the euro area crisis.

Except the ECB was not a normal central bank. Nor, despite its own obsession with theory and doctrine, could it see that it required a new theory about its own role if the euro area were to survive. Its peculiar identity, combined with its anxieties about its own balance sheet, were stopping it from fulfilling the role the IMF would expect of a central bank. These unresolved issues made for a challenging working relationship when the ECB and IMF finally came together in the Troika. But in the course of learning to work together, not only did they update the crisis management rule book, they found a way to save the euro.

Lesson #7: Finding a voice for a crisis.

In the Spring of 1996, I was sharing a house with a Newcastle United supporter and a Manchester United supporter. It was the fourth season of the English Premier League and Kevin Keegan, the Newcastle manager, was leading his team towards its first top-tier title since 1927. There was a palpable optimism among Magpie fans, including my otherwise cautious Geordie housemate. So when, on a night of pulsating action and drama on 3 April, Liverpool beat Newcastle 4-3, my housemate's world started to fall apart. Newcastle had fallen further behind the Red Devils. The title looked like it might have gone for good.

The result against Liverpool was only the beginning of his torment. My Manchester United supporting housemate, Nick, had maintained a dignified and sympathetic silence during the match. But even he was unable to contain himself three weeks later when, despite a Newcastle victory at Leeds United, Kevin Keegan imploded on national television. Nick looked across the room and said, 'That's it then. It's over for Newcastle, and it's over for Keegan.'

He was right on both counts. Not only had Newcastle surrendered a twelve point lead at the end of January, Keegan was losing a psychological battle with the Manchester United manager, Alex Ferguson. In the minds of Newcastle supporters, the club's diminishing advantage had, by April, become a crisis. And their leader, the passionate and beloved Keegan, was failing to locate that calm and authoritative voice which might have quelled their doubts, not to mention salvage the championship. By contrast, Ferguson was mastering the art of saying not very much. When he did speak, his words had the right impact on those in his own dressing room, and in the minds of his opponents. It may not have been pretty, but it was effective.

Ferguson's and Keegan's contrasting styles spoke to deeper truths about their personalities. There was always a sense during the 1995-1996 season that Keegan never quite knew his own mind. He made some impulsive player purchases which disrupted his team at crucial points in the campaign. He also rose to Ferguson's bait, which not only unsettled him, but undoubtedly had the same effect on his dressing room. The club's leader look rattled, and in a crisis this does nothing to promote confidence.

Ferguson could not have been more different. By 1996, he was a voice of authority, someone admired and respected for his achievements. Not only *what* he achieved but *how* he achieved his objectives. The Manchester United manager self-evidently knew what he wanted, as well as how to get it. He had long since worked out how to lead in a high pressure environment. How to operate in a role where he was under constant scrutiny, and how to deal with the advice which always comes, unbidden, to a leader.

Because leaders are rarely short of advice, they have to work out what matters. And the arbiter of quality must be the leader himself. What are the objectives which must be pursued? Which activities are essential to the achievement of these objectives? Who are the key people? Without this *a priori* filter, advice can overwhelm or paralyse a leader, especially in a crisis. Ferguson knew this, Keegan did not.

We sometimes ascribe this ability to a leader's possession of an 'inner voice'. This is not, of course, observable. But where there is no inner voice, there will certainly be no outer one. Ireland was fortunate to have two presidents in succession who, since they had strong inner voices, found strong outer ones. They did so during a period in Irish history when it mattered that the occupant of Áras an Uachtaráin had moral authority. During the Troubles, Mary Robinson was able to address more than one community on a divided island. Mary McAleese, her successor, did the same, notably when she spoke powerfully on behalf of the nation during Queen Elizabeth II's historic visit to Ireland in 2011.

This trip occurred as the embers of the financial crisis were still smouldering in Dublin, and after Irish prestige had taken a knock. The speeches the respective Heads of State delivered at Dublin Castle were minor masterpieces, combining wisdom, empathy and historical understanding. The words were spoken by two extraordinary women. But the voices were those of remarkable leaders. They managed to articulate the importance of the bonds between two nations whose shared history has not always been a happy one.

This had taken decades of practice for Elizabeth Windsor and Mary McAleese. Over time they learned to speak on behalf of nations, to find the voice their roles demanded. Another female leader, Margaret Thatcher, literally changed her voice. Under the guidance of her supporters in the 1970s, she received voice coaching. The immediate result was to lower her register. The enduring consequence was to implant a recognisable voice of authority into the centre of British political life and the nation's consciousness.

But none of these female leaders plucked their leadership voice from thin air. Nor did they find a way through the thicket of advice and advisors by chance. They each possessed strong convictions, which themselves were rooted in strong values. They were also sufficiently self-aware to be able to judge what to say and how to say it at the appropriate time. They were able to use their voice of authority authoritatively.

A leader's voice relates to their words as a conductor of an orchestra relates to a composer's score. The words themselves are important, but anyone watching or hearing a leader speak will pay as much, if not more, attention to how their words are spoken. The logical, thinking part of our brain will parse the words. The more immediate, emotional part of our nature will focus on the unspoken signals, whether they are intended or not. In this respect, a leader's voice can be about what is not said, and how it is left unsaid, as much as it is about the words.

We very quickly stop listening to those leaders who appear to have swallowed, rather than kissed, the Blarney Stone.

The unspoken emotional and physical dimension of a leader's voice is sometimes called 'poise' or 'gravitas'. It is assumed that the individual who can display these characteristics, particularly under pressure, has mastered their emotions. It would be more accurate to say they have understood their own emotions, and those of the people around them. This is something more profound than a matter of empathy. It suggests an ability to understand why the emotions exist in the first place. Such emotionally intelligent people more easily find the right voice.

And the right voice counts for a lot in a crisis. In a somewhat unfair, but nonetheless penetrating quip, the Irish economist, Colm McCarthy, made this very point when he described the appearance of Ireland's Financial Regulator on national television in 2008. Quoted in a piece Michael Lewis wrote for *Vanity Fair*, McCarthy said, 'What happened was that everyone in Ireland had the idea that somewhere in Ireland there was a little wise old man who was in charge of the money, and this was the first time they'd ever seen this little man. And then they saw him and said "who the f*** was that?" That's when everyone panicked'. As Financial Regulator, Patrick Neary failed to locate the voice he required, and that was required of his role, at this crucial moment in Irish history.

❄   ❄   ❄

As we discovered during the COVID-19 pandemic, the most compelling leadership came from those figures who were able to talk confidently about the realities of the outbreak in a humane, compassionate yet realistic manner. The grim statistics spoke for themselves. We did not require a cold analysis of what these figures meant, an accountant's presentation of the viral profit and loss account. We wanted emotionally intelligent, right-brain descriptions of left-brain solutions. Nor did we want confident yet false assurances. We could all see the situation was highly uncertain and troubling. Those leaders who read the psychological demands of the moment, who found their voice for a crisis, proved the most convincing.

And caring is an indispensable condition in crisis management. Few will voluntarily follow the leader who does not care for the problem or for them. They will question their motivation, their judgement. Even when we do not realise it, we are looking beyond the words to what people actually do. What their facial muscles betray about what they are feeling. What their body language is like when they give us news. These are tried and tested ways to find out who someone really is as a person, and therefore whether they are to be trusted to lead.

We saw the best and worst of our leaders during the COVID-19 pandemic. Those who were able to relate to the concerns of citizens. Those who found a way to talk about the gravity of the crisis without sounding defensive, on the one hand, or alarmist on the other. Those who managed to appeal to our better instincts in support of extraordinary measures. Those able to explain the *why*, not just the what or how. Those leaders who had sufficient confidence to admit they had made mistakes.

Our frame of reference has to take account of how different leaders reacted as the crisis unfolded. But as time passes we may place more emphasis on what happened, or more accurately did not happen, before the outbreak. We will also want to understand what is going to be done to limit the economic damage and prevent a recurrence. Will those leaders who were able to speak to their citizens persuasively during the lockdown be the same people who improve public health systems, who foster greater international cooperation and who prepare for the next crisis?

Following previous crises, leaders have emerged who have rebuilt, reformed and strengthened economies and societies, who have given a voice to progress. One of the most enduring examples of post-crisis reconstruction was the Marshall Plan. Following the calamity of the Second World War, the US mobilised itself to rebuild Europe. Equally, one only has to read the Founding Charter of the United Nations to grasp that generation's moral seriousness, its evident desire to make the world a better place.

Although COVID-19 has wrought considerably less damage than the conflict of 1939-1945, we need to rebuild and strengthen our collective defences. We will discover in the coming decade whether we are blessed with leaders who can, in the best sense of the term, give voice to this mission.

Some lessons for leaders in a crisis:

1. **Find out what people feel, not just what they think.**
   A crisis changes many of our settled assumptions: about people, organisations and our own place in the world. A leader will not be short of advice based on what people *think* about the new, crisis-induced reality. The challenge is to grasp how people feel, to comprehend the emotional reaction to dislocation. This is necessary in order to calibrate a credible, persuasive response.

2. **It is possible to lead with conviction in an uncertain situation.** If a leader wants others to believe in a certain course of action, they have to demonstrate they believe it themselves. The challenge in a crisis is that it is very hard to be certain about the future. But a leader can demonstrate commitment, resolution and fortitude without being certain, and do so while also levelling with people about the effects of uncertainty. This is a matter of tone, and as such part of the leader's voice.

3. **Meet expectations, do not be crushed by them.** It is not necessary to read books about leadership to realise they set unrealistic expectations of leaders. The sort of superhuman qualities leaders are expected to develop seem to make little allowance for the realities of being human. A crisis only increases these expectations. To be effective in a crisis, a leader needs to acknowledge these expectations, but not be crushed by them. Your reaction to pressure will be very evident to others in your voice.

8.

Making a Troika

There was great excitement in the kitchen of Rasam, a distinguished Indian restaurant in Glasthule, a suburb in south Dublin. The IMF was coming for dinner. And not just the IMF. Its famous Indian head of mission, the suave and thoughtful Ajai Chopra, was dining that evening. Rasam was not official Indian territory, but it was the next closest thing in Dublin after the Indian Embassy. Tired of hotel food, and needing to be reminded of his home country's cuisine, Ajai decided it was time he and his team enjoyed a curry.

Dublin is a city of few secrets and news of the IMF's visit to Rasam spread. It did a lot to help the IMF's public image. Most of us can relate to the need for a curry and a few beers after a long day. Indulging in one of life's great culinary pleasures humanised these exotic, if distant, officials from Washington, DC. Ajai's gracious conduct on the evening itself also helped. The manager told me how it had touched the restaurant's staff. This only added to the aura which developed around Ajai. The media quickly latched onto the charismatic Indian, perhaps believing their audience might get a better sense of the IMF through one of its personalities. He therefore became the public face of a bailout. Photographers

were happy to tail him across Dublin. He was regularly pho-
tographed smiling in a warm yet slightly shy manner. This
fed a perception that he must be in Dublin to help. Someone
who carried himself in this way did not look like he wanted
to return Ireland to the Middle Ages. That he did not say
very much did not seem to matter. If anything, it added to his
status as an oracle. He was well suited to a country attracted,
and some might say susceptible, to charm and charisma.

Ajai's smile took the edge off the IMF's famously austere
brand. It also contrasted with the generally unsmiling and
somewhat stiff posture of officials from the European Commission and European Central Bank. These were the three
organisations who comprised the Troika, the euro area's
answer to the crises which had engulfed Greece, Ireland and
Portugal.

The name 'Troika' became a talking point in its own right.
It sounded like a Soviet-era term because it *was* a Soviet-era
term. It referred to those brief interludes when a group of
senior party officials took charge following the death of the
Communist Party's General Secretary. Whether it was a
conscious choice or not, it conjured all sorts of memories
of Kremlin intrigue and the brutal exercise of power. And
the reborn Troika was certainly powerful. At a time when
the Irish State could not fund itself, the Troika was the only
thing standing between Dublin and default. It was not a state
in its own right. It did not have a territory. Nor did it have an
army. But it could raise money, and it had a mandate from
the world's most powerful governments.

The Troika landed in a blaze of publicity, but shrouded
in mystery. Many blithely assumed it had the whip hand,
and that Dublin would tamely fall into line. But this did not

happen. I do not think anyone quite realised that this process was going to run on very Irish rails from the beginning. And not because the Irish state had a Machiavellian master plan up its sleeves. On the contrary, the Irish instinct to play it straight disarmed officials from the Troika. No tricks. No games. It did not take long for trusting relationships to form between Dublin and the Troika. Those traditions of state-craft familiar to major powers, but largely unfamiliar to Irish officials, worked in Ireland's favour.

But much had happened in the months before it arrived. During the autumn of 2010, the State's funding position had become ever more precarious in government bond markets. Speculation about a rescue grew. Fearing the inevitable political repercussions, the government denied the possibility of a bailout. But still the speculation continued. Expectations grew of an announcement from the government. Hints were dropped to the media that discussions were taking place. But nothing was confirmed.

Nor could it have been confirmed. This would have pulled the rug out from under the feet of officials negotiating with the Troika. Kevin Cardiff was adamant in meetings during November that since no formal request for assistance had been made, nothing could be agreed. On 10 November 2010, one of the first fact-finding calls took place, with the Troika dialling-into a call from Washington, Brussels and Frankfurt. It was not quite the cast of *Ben Hur*, but there were enough officials from the European Commission, ECB and IMF to make it a long and drawn out experience.

We left this call, as we left most encounters with the Troika, with a sackful of requests for data. But these were a distraction at a time when pressure on the banks was reaching new levels of intensity. The media reported on 11 November that the IMF was considering burden sharing with depositors. This triggered a reaction. The normally unflappable Michael Maher, from the Central Bank team which managed our loans to the banks, appeared outside my office looking nervous. He said we were receiving reports from every corner of Ireland of people withdrawing money. It illustrated the fragility of the system.

The Irish authorities spent 12 November in a day-long huddle. There was an urgent need to develop the Irish 'ask' of the Troika. There was an equally pressing desire to avoid making any commitments which might tie the government's hands. During a call later in the afternoon, the ECB was more than usually belligerent in its demands. It had evidently picked up on the reports of deposit outflows. It saw them as a threat to its own position, as sucking it further into the Irish mire. But in a welcome intervention, the IMF took the opposing view. Perhaps worried that its burden sharing slip-up might identify it as the hardline party in the Troika, it came out against repaying the ECB in the near term. The battle lines within the Troika were being drawn.

But as the hours passed, the pressure continued to build. It was only a matter of time before a bailout would have to be announced. In the normal course of events, a lectern, with flanking tricolours, would have been assembled on the steps of Government Buildings. There would have been solemn yet defiant speeches from elected politicians. But this is not how it happened. The nation found out while poised peacefully over its breakfast cereal when Patrick Honohan, who was at Frankfurt airport on the end of a mobile phone, appeared impromptu on *Morning Ireland*, RTÉ's flagship news radio programme.

He might have been phoning his wife to tell her about a delayed flight. Instead, he was telling the nation that help was on its way. Although he introduced some conditionality at the end of his call by suggesting the government had a choice whether to accept a bailout, he had more or less revealed what was going to happen in the next act of the drama. His meaning was clear, as were the consequences for the State. It was an extraordinary moment.

An immediate effect, beyond the dropping of a million teaspoons, was to cause much phoning around among officials. I certainly had to tell myself I had heard him correctly. In Dame Street, many others were similarly dumbfounded. The Central Bank's press office pulled a recording together so we could listen again. Even Patrick's professorial hesitation could not obscure the message. The IMF was coming to Ireland.

A handful of us had been keeping the possibility of a bailout under our hats for weeks. Not long before Patrick addressed *Morning Ireland*, he and other officials, including Matthew, had attended a secret meeting with the nascent Troika team in Brussels. On 14 November, they had flown out and back from the military airbase at Baldonnel on the Irish government jet. On his return, Matthew briefed me on the discussions. He explained that while the ECB remained fixated on bank deleveraging, the IMF indicated it was inclined to be more pragmatic on this issue. But on the key question of the government's parlous finances, the talks were no more than exploratory. They could not be otherwise. Although we were close to a bailout, there was no way Kevin,

Patrick or anyone else could put the State into the hands of the IMF without the government's consent. It could not, in turn, make the decision until the broad parameters of an agreement were settled. This was not achieved in Brussels.

Patrick's announcement had the same relieving effect as a thunder storm on an intolerably humid day. Confidence in the already damaged banking system was draining fast. There was open talk of a government default. The gap between the government's claimed reality and Ireland's actual situation was massive. The government had hoped for a while that incremental changes might avoid a bailout. But we had long since passed that point. A grand gesture was required. Nothing else would do. The State could not finance itself. The banks were in the same position. The economy was contracting. The government lacked any credibility. A new story needed to be written about Ireland.

So when Patrick told the Irish people what the government would not, he opened a new chapter. The IMF, with all of its experience of crises, certainly understood the importance of stories. It knew that people needed to believe something new and different about Ireland. And in its principal spokesman, Ajai Chopra, it had someone capable of articulating this message. He did not shy away from saying that some nasty medicine needed to be swallowed. But his bedside manner took some of the edge off its taste.

What it could not do was extinguish genuine concerns about the power the Troika wielded, nor address questions about its accountability. Its officials were unelected. They were going to make decisions which would have a material impact on the lives of Irish citizens. It was perfectly reasonable to ask about the rights of ordinary Irish people.

It was also entirely fair to question how the Troika would make decisions. Ireland is a parliamentary democracy. The country's politicians and officials are publicly accountable for their actions. The Troika was going to operate behind closed doors. While this was necessary for progress to be made, the resulting opacity only fuelled the suspicions of those who saw Irish democracy being upended. The ECB had already thrown its weight around in Ireland. Would the EC and IMF do the same?

It did not help that Ireland entered the process from a position of weakness. But the deck was not completely stacked against Dublin. The Troika structure was novel yet untested. It was far from being the unified force the name implied and the media's coverage suggested. Each of its three members had its own interests and priorities. The personal chemistry between the respective leaders of the three institutions was professional rather than warm. There was much greater alignment among the Irish team. On the big issues, it was impossible to squeeze a cigarette paper between Kevin and Patrick. At moments, there was a tobacco plantation between Brussels, Frankfurt and Washington, DC.

These divisions revealed themselves early. In the lead for the IMF was the astute and direct Ashoka Mody. He arrived in Dublin carrying some damage from a gunshot wound. It was hard not to be transfixed as he delivered a coherent, if damning, assessment of the mishandling of the euro area crisis. Here was someone from outside Ireland more or less saying what we had been for months. In doing so, he immediately provided a counterweight to the ECB's diagnosis, as well as its prescription. Not only did he question the ECB's stance on deleveraging and deflation, he articulated an alternative view of what the ECB could do if it changed its approach.

After months of pressure from the ECB, Ashoka Mody's alternative perspective was welcome. We could safely infer from his comments that the ECB was not going to get its own way within the Troika. It suggested that alternative proposals from the Irish side would get a fair hearing. It also indicated that the IMF was not going to let the ECB escape its responsibilities as Ireland's central bank. Mody did not mince his words: the ECB's interests were best served by supporting the Irish banks so the Irish State could put its own house in order. He made this point forcefully in 2010. (He made it again in 2018, in his magisterial survey of the euro area crisis, *EuroTragedy: A Drama in Nine Acts*.) He also did nothing to hide his belief that Ireland should compel better terms from Frankfurt. He was adamant it could do so. One of his stock metaphors involved Irish hands attaching to Frankfurt's sensitive parts and squeezing hard. Refreshing in its clarity, Mody's analysis gave hope to the Irish side that the IMF would be an ally. It did, of course, have to operate within the constraints of a Troika process which demanded cohesion. But they knew, as we knew, that parents do not always agree. There was a gap to be exploited.

Ashoka Mody's presentation had the further merit of leaving no one within the Troika having to guess the IMF's stance. Similarly, Klaus Masuch's muscular assessment of Ireland's responsibilities left little doubt as to how Frankfurt viewed the world. Such a fundamental difference of opinion hardly seemed the most secure foundation for their new partnership.

There are times, though, when sharp differences of opinion lead to the resolution of an issue, as long as they are expressed openly and honestly. All four participants to the process had a view, and there were opportunities for each to have its say. These early discussions allowed progress to be made, and key areas to be pinpointed. And so rather than dancing around the central issue of debt sustainability, this quickly became the focus. This had been the point of disagreement between the ECB and Dublin for months, with the Irish authorities adamant that, given time, repayment of ECB loans would occur. The IMF's involvement ended the Irish authorities' lonely advocacy of the *when* not *if* argument. This was welcome to Irish officials. Dublin wanted a solution. It was not enjoying the adversarial relationship with Frankfurt. So when the possibility of a compromise opened up, in part due to the IMF's early interventions, Irish officials were quick to occupy this ground. All of a sudden, officials could start to work on those practical measures which might bring the crisis to a conclusion.

The main problem to be resolved was the State's financial condition. The Troika's members agreed among themselves on this issue, and the Irish authorities agreed with the Troika. So having settled *what* had to be done, the emphasis shifted to *how* it could be done. In broad terms, there were two areas of focus: the public finances and the banks. Although the banks were blamed for the government's financial situation, they were only part of the story. The public finances were not in great condition before Ireland went into the crisis, with the tax base too geared to receipts from the property boom, among other drawbacks. Although it was convenient for the government to pin the blame on the banks, this distorted the reality of poor fiscal discipline in the 2000s. The Troika's Economic Adjustment Programme for Ireland involved cuts to public expenditure. But it also involved a reshaping of the public finances to address the earlier weaknesses. There could be no question that the banks had made a difficult problem worse. Yet it was far from the whole story.

The banks were, of course, the Central Bank's responsibility. We knew a lot about them after a difficult year of stress tests and probing examinations. So when the Troika arrived in Dublin, it encountered a group who knew Anglo, AIB, Bank of Ireland, EBS and Permanent TSB inside out. We did not have all the answers. Nor could we afford the ones we did have. Yet much of the research and development work, on which the Troika would later come to rely, had been done. The Troika pressed the accelerator when it was required, but the chassis we needed for the coming journey had already been built.

And it was this team which, in November 2010, started to plan the second Irish stress test. This was the make-or-break centrepiece of a broader initiative to tackle the problems in the banking system: the Financial Measures Programme. Anticipation levels were high as there had already been two attempts to break the toxic link between the State and the banks, neither of which had been successful. Few, including the Troika, were confident that the Financial Measures Programme could be delivered in the available time. It would cost tens of millions of euros, involve hundreds of people, and was devilishly complex. We knew it was high risk, and we knew it was the last shot in our locker.

Lesson #8: It is very hard to fix a problem you created.

Towards the end of his life, the former US defence secretary, Robert McNamara, reviewed his life on camera for the documentary *Fog of War*. In an otherwise glittering career, the Vietnam War stained his record and his conscience. In the film, the former Harvard MBA graduate expresses his deep regret at decisions he made about the conduct of the conflict. He draws eleven lessons from his experiences. These comprise the misjudgements and mistakes that led to millions of deaths, the near destruction of a country and ultimate American defeat and withdrawal from Vietnam. In powerful closing testimony, McNamara concedes that reason has limits, and that leaders need to be prepared to re-examine their reasoning.

One of the things which makes McNamara's self-examination so extraordinary is that we are unused to seeing leaders describing where they went wrong. It is also compelling because McNamara locates a pattern of behaviour in government whereby decision-making errors compounded. This meant that the negative effects of policies were amplified, leading, in the Vietnam War, to the loss of more lives, and making it harder for the US to extract itself from the conflict. The authors of the *Harvard Business Review* article, 'The Hidden Traps in Decision Making', called this phenomenon the Sunk Cost Trap. They suggest it shows up with 'disturbing regularity' in banking. This is because bankers, unwilling to acknowledge a poor lending decision, will advance more money to a business in trouble in the hope that it will recover. It is the same behaviour, in essence, which stops us walking out of the cinema during an appalling film. We tell ourselves we have paid for something, and therefore we ought to extract value from the experience

The global financial crisis was characterised by a series of such compounding errors. It was also characterised by the near complete absence of any recognition of, or repentance for, these errors. When mistakes were admitted, it was striking by virtue of being exceptional. James Crosby, the former chief executive of the failed Halifax Bank of Scotland, made a heartfelt apology, handed back some of his pension, and offered to relinquish his knighthood. His counterpart at RBS, Fred Goodwin, did none of these things, reinforcing the perception that he never accepted responsibility for his part in that bank's downfall.

There are lots of lessons to be drawn from the different paths Crosby and Goodwin followed. But the ones on which the media and politicians focused at the time, such as who caused the bigger mess, or who displayed greater contrition, were of little importance in the middle of the crisis. A lot of emotional energy was invested in debates about punishment of bankers. What actually mattered, in the white heat of the crisis, was whether incumbent bankers, assuming their credibility was not fatally damaged, could rebuild viable banks. Whether or not former bankers saw the error of their ways, or might even be prosecuted, had little bearing on whether the system could be cleaned-up more quickly. Retribution and blame do not end a crisis.

In fact, they complicate the task of crisis management. Under pressure from the media and politicians, officials divert resources towards backward-looking investigations, and away from activities designed to repair the damage. And those who are being criticised publicly start to behave differently, and sometimes in ways which only makes it harder for them to do their job. This is one of the unavoidable psychological consequences of being involved in failure. It affects how people feel about themselves, how they believe people see them, and it can lead to a downward spiral in self-esteem. But some struggle to accept responsibility and so blame others, or seek to deflect criticism. Some go a stage further and try to cover their tracks. A handful, recognising their own mistakes, set about trying to repair the damage. During the global financial crisis, I met a lot of disorientated individuals, each of them struggling to deal with failure and criticism, and each finding it hard to become part of the solution to that crisis.

Criticism is hard to receive even when things are going well. But in a crisis, when a lifetime of work might have been swept away, it will trigger the sort of profound emotional responses which follow grief. This is why denial, the first stage of the grief cycle, is such a common reaction. We know that something bad has happened as a consequence of a crisis, but we wish to avoid the pain of confronting a new reality. In this denial phase, there is every temptation to pretend that things are not as bad as they might seem. When this happens we can quickly become an obstruction, even where this is not our intention. Unable to cope with the new situation, we become absorbed in trying to understand why things changed.

When this happens, we are not focused on the issues at hand, we are looking back. The right answer for the individual, and their new colleagues, may well be to find them an alternative role, or even move them out of the organisation.

But this should be handled very carefully. A blame culture serves no one, least of all the person blaming (or being seen to blame) others. It will simply create an environment of fear, distort decisions in a different way, and possibly even work against the objectives trying to be achieved.

A crisis creates a psychological border between old and new realities. We cross it many times, and therefore we may be unable to perceive how our world has changed. One of the biggest challenges in the Irish crisis was to get the banks to face the realities of their loan books. This mattered as we could not establish an accurate picture of the losses until it happened. It also mattered as we needed the banks to recover value from these loan books to preserve capital. But many of the people doing this work were the same people who had made the bad loans in the first place. And it turned out that too many of them were in denial about the reality they had created. This slowed the process of recovery.

As Richard Wodehouse demonstrated through his pursuit of the Quinn Group, and Anglo's other major exposures, when new people took on the task of loan recovery, they made more progress, more quickly. If I had to do it all again, I would make sure there were people able to do this work available much earlier. I would also try to convince the government that it was in its interests to allow these people to make a decent return from their work. It is a paradox of the Irish crisis that banks, who achieved massive rewards for originating poor loans on the way down, were restricted from paying people who recovered value, often against the odds, on the way up. This undoubtedly slowed the process of recovering value, and it led to a less good outcome for the taxpayer.

❄   ❄   ❄

This ought to be at the front of officials' minds as the economic clean-up begins following the COVID-19 pandemic. No one can be blamed for creating the economic damage. However, the same skills which countries, including Ireland, required after the global financial crisis will be needed again. Good businesses will otherwise go to the wall. Loans will become unnecessarily impaired. Leadership in this area of crisis recovery will be even more important after the pandemic than the global financial crisis. Governments should organise themselves accordingly as there is an urgent need to recover lost output and prevent business failures.

But what of the public health issues? How can lessons be learned in a way which strengthens the resilience of health-care systems?

Fresh eyes will be needed after the pandemic as they were needed after the financial crisis. In the same way that it was hard for incumbent financial regulators to see where things had gone wrong before the crisis, so it will be hard for some public health officials to revisit their own assumptions and decisions. New leaders will be needed, and institutions will need to be reformed. This can strengthen a system. But it requires vision and strong political leadership.

We also require political leaders who will not indulge in superficial debates, and who will not pursue makeshift remedies. Unlike the global financial crisis, there are no obvious or easy targets to serve as a focal point for criticism after the pandemic. This is a good thing, but it will not prevent some people trying to label particular countries, institutions or individuals as being at fault, just as bankers and regulators were blamed after 2008. It is therefore likely new targets will emerge, new scapegoats will be found. But no challenge as complex as the pandemic can be understood by parading villains, any more than cheap shots at bankers shed light on the origins of the financial crisis. Following such a serious disruption to the normal functioning of societies and economies, we cannot afford to deflect attention from the real issues by indulging in a political Punch and Judy show.

Following the global financial crisis, thoughtful political leaders were largely able to avoid the blame game and focus on the issues which mattered. This allowed the financial system to be reformed and repaired. We will find out whether the political class of the 2020s can provide equivalent leadership. Only when we reliably understand what should have been done before the pandemic, and during its early phases, can we start to think about reform. And hard as it may be to accept, some of the officials who have worked incredibly hard during the COVID-19 outbreak may not be the right people to rebuild public health structures. Equally, some of the institutions on which we thought we could rely, at a national and international level, may not be fit for the future. Fresh thinking is required, and its most likely source is fresh blood, unencumbered by those errors and omissions which, as Robert McNamara observed, compound due to no more than the passage of time.

Some lessons for leaders in a crisis:

1. **There are different categories of mistakes, different types of errors.** If a crisis is the result of omissions and

errors, it is often resolved through a series of mistakes. Ireland only escaped its crisis after a series of wrong turns and occasional misjudgements. But these were, for the most part, recognised at the time, and a course correction occurred. A leader will make mistakes in a crisis, but these will only represent a failure if they are not acknowledged and the consequences addressed at the time.

2. **Bring problems to the surface quickly**. There is a tendency for us to believe that we understand the totality of the issues we face at a given point in time. This presents all sorts of risks in a crisis, not least that we overlook problems which later surface and cause damage. A leader needs to prevent this by ensuring that previously unknown problems are identified and understood. And where they observe someone obstructing this discovery process, consciously or not, that individual needs to re-assigned.

3. **Avoiding a blame culture**. Although there may be a need to change personnel in order to tackle a crisis, problems will not be solved if people conclude they will be punished for taking risks and making honest mistakes. The leader needs to be realistic about who is and who is not helping. But how they implement these decisions matters since they will be a signal to others. A blame culture will be incredibly debilitating and impede work to end a crisis.

9.

The Mother of All Stress Tests

'The Department of Finance represents the government and people of Ireland. The Central Bank does not.'

I had only just finished speaking when these words tumbled from the mouth of a previously unseen Department of Finance official. I wasn't sure whether to laugh or put my head in my hands. I looked across the table at the Troika. I could see they were more amused than alarmed. One of them caught my eye. He raised an eyebrow as if to ask what was going on. But he did not look surprised. This moment had been brewing for a few weeks.

We were at Dame Street for another meeting of Irish officials and the Troika. In the weeks before the meeting, the Central Bank had developed its thinking on the future of the banking system. We knew we had an opportunity to make some far-reaching changes to the banks and the regulatory regime. Since we did not want to waste it, we had gathered our ideas in what we were calling the Financial Measures Programme. This had wrong-footed the Department of Finance who, for perfectly good reasons of their own, were less ambitious about reform. But someone at the department had obviously decided that enough was enough and had despatched a messenger. As I had not met the department's mystery representative on the way into the meeting, I asked some colleagues if they knew him. They did. They said they were unsurprised given his reputation.

The official's clumsy intervention came at one of the regular start-of-mission meetings with the Troika. These show-and-tell sessions were an opportunity for the Irish authorities to explain progress against the objectives of the programme. They gave the Troika a chance to assess work completed, as well as gauge the Irish team's state of mind. These meetings mattered. How we conducted ourselves therefore mattered. I chaired most of them myself as I tended to be the most senior Irish official in the room. I believed that we were likely to get more out of them if they were relaxed occasions. I also believed we would only gain the Troika's trust if we were open and collegiate. This meant not behaving as if the Troika was our opposition. For this reason, the department's display of muscle sent all of the wrong signals. We had to work with the Troika, and we had to work with each other, but all of a sudden we looked defensive and disjointed.

I told Matthew and Patrick later that day what had happened. Both men grimaced. They had been in the meeting of the Troika principals at more or less the same time. This group comprised the most senior officials from Dublin and the Troika. Although it did not include politicians, Kevin and Patrick acted with reference to the government. Elected officials would always take the major decisions.

The principals spent most of their time discussing Ireland's public finances. This was the key issue as it determined what could be done elsewhere, not least for the banks. At the end of each mission, the Troika summarised the outputs from all of these meetings in a published progress update. These updates were very important as they allowed us to tell a different story about Ireland.

But what story did we want to tell? There was no clear answer in November 2010. Although the Fianna Fáil administration was on its last legs, it remained in charge. The Troika's arrival was humiliating enough. The government had little appetite for a far-reaching reform programme, not least as it would have implied it had not been doing its job. But sweeping reform was required. Ireland had experienced a major failure of economic governance in the 2000s (and arguably long before). The banking system was a mess. The regulatory regime needed an overhaul. The Troika's arrival was an opportunity to reform the system.

This was not a good crisis by any stretch of the imagination, but it was one not to be wasted. Ireland had developed a successful, open economy over decades. This included the dynamic International Financial Services Centre which other European capitals eyed with a mixture of envy and hostility. To remain an attractive destination for foreign investment, Ireland needed to demonstrate that it was willing to change. It needed to demonstrate it was a serious, well-governed country. The Troika's arrival created the opportunity to do these things. All of a sudden, there was a chance to get things done. To overcome decades of inertia. To tackle the vested interests which everyone knew existed. To address the perception that some of Ireland's problems were due to it being a country of only four million people.

The Department of Finance, in its more conservative moments, seemed to take the view that the task was to put the Irish train back onto its existing rails. Perhaps the crisis had worn down those officials who might, at a different time, have pursued a reforming vision for their country. There was a feeling of resignation among some civil servants. A largely unspoken belief that Ireland was destined to operate in a certain way. Even those who hoped for change saw obstacles in the way the political class operated. But as it was self-evident that the crisis had exposed the limitations of the political system in Ireland, it was hard to see the case for tinkering at the margins. Where was the great reforming vision for the Irish State within the Irish civil service? A decade later and the consequences of this lack of ambition can be seen in housing, healthcare, transport and other areas of Irish life where bold, long-term solutions are still required.

As an outsider, it was easier for me to say these things. I had not spent years trying to navigate the Irish political system and government bureaucracy. For those on the inside, there was understandable apprehension about the Troika. Some officials therefore tried to limit the Troika's influence. In their view, the Troika had a limited role: to do no more than relieve the pressures on the public finances. The idea that the Troika might be involved in wider areas of policy was anathema. But for those officials who had agitated for change, the Troika's arrival was an opportunity to secure reforms needed for years. Matthew and I certainly saw things this way.

Even though I had spent a lot of time with him in the months since my arrival, and had got to know him well, I still found Matthew hard to read at times. His demeanour was more or less the same whether we were discussing the weekend's football results or the latest revelations from one of the banks. So I was surprised when, one afternoon, he asked me, out of the blue, to lead the Financial Measures Programme. He said that he and Patrick had discussed what they thought needed to happen. They both agreed that they wanted me to make it happen.

Only a matter of months before, we had both been outsiders. We moved to Ireland for our own reasons. Neither of us had expected to be caught up in a sovereign debt crisis. Now the future of this system was, to a degree, in our hands. This made us, to a certain extent, insiders, and we both felt emotionally vested in the enterprise. We had an opportunity to make a difference to something which we both believed mattered. We were both enjoying ourselves, and we were ready to deliver the reforms which would comprise the Financial Measures Programme.

The following day, Matthew and I met Patrick to discuss the approach we would take to the programme. The objective was simple: to remove any doubts about the current health and long-term viability of the banking system. If this could be done, and the cost of doing so quantified convincingly, the uncertainty surrounding the expense to the State could be removed. As the State now had a backstop in the Troika, and so did not need to rely on funding markets, the focus would then shift to the affordability of loans from the IMF and other sources. On paper, the logic which underpinned this approach was deceptively simple. But we all knew the banks remained the weak link. Not even the banks themselves knew what was really sitting on their balance sheets. Until this information was available, and until it was reliable, the banks would pose a threat to the recovery efforts.

This was certainly Patrick's main concern. He had thought long and hard about this issue. He did not trust the banks.

Although this did not distinguish him from any other Irish citizen, his distrust was for practical rather than emotional reasons. He simply did not believe they were in control of their own numbers. He also had some scars from the earlier stress test. Perhaps this was in his mind that afternoon as he was uncharacteristically direct. He said we would all be looking for new jobs if we flunked this second test. This was not a threat. Patrick did not make threats. It was the honest assessment of a self-effacing public servant.

As he started to describe his priorities for the test, it quickly dawned on me that this was going to be a larger and more complicated exercise than before. He said we had no choice but to involve third parties given the tight deadline. He also suggested the Central Bank needed its own advisers to guide on bank restructuring and loan sales. Rothschild, the investment bank, had been working for the Department of Finance since the early days of the crisis. I had seen John Kingman, the former UK Treasury official now working for Rothschild, a few times at Merrion Street. Patrick thought the Central Bank required an equivalent sounding board as we debated what to do with the banks and the problem loans in the system.

Patrick knew this would be expensive, but he wanted to signal that Dame Street was serious about the exercise. We discussed the inherent difficulties of a project much broader and deeper than the March 2010 stress test. We needed to establish definitively the costs of dealing with the problem loans. We needed to develop options for disposing of these loans. We had to put in place a credible funding plan for banks heavily reliant on central bank lending. We were therefore going to need help to manage this project. I sensed that Patrick and Matthew were both doubtful about the end of March deadline. As was I, but I also believed in the importance of sounding confident in adversity. I assured them we could do what needed to be done by the end of the first quarter. It was not a bluff, but I did not leave the room completely certain about the commitment I had just made.

When I next discussed all of these issues with Matthew and Patrick, there was not an immediate consensus about where we should focus our time and energies. I did not believe we could simply re-tread the same ground as the March exercise, only in more depth. There were too many questions about the viability of individual banks, which was an issue of funding, capital and market structure. For this reason, I argued that, as well as looking at the viability of individual banks, we needed to look at the system as a whole. Matthew and Patrick were less sure. They saw solvency as the overriding issue, with the management of the problem loans the secondary concern. Too great a focus on funding and viability could, they reasoned, distract our attention. We debated these points over the coming weeks. I stuck to my guns, and as I spoke to more people, especially the team at Barclays Capital, I concluded that unless we had a clear message about how the banks would make money, any fresh injection of capital, however significant, might prove no more than a stopgap. We needed to address head-on the genuine concerns about the viability of the banks.

This was, of course, a solvency issue. Weak banks are less likely to attract funding. But I had never bought the argument that simply putting more capital into the banks would be sufficient. We needed to explain how the banks would fund current and future lending profitably. We could not expect wholesale funding markets to magically open to Irish banks. In fact, it was clear that banks across the world were going to have to rely less on wholesale markets. Irish banks were not immune from the development. As such, they would be more reliant on domestic deposits than they had been in the past. But the banking system had long since outgrown the supply of such funds. This had left the banks with high loan-to-deposit ratios. As the crisis developed, this metric had been an increasingly troubling one for markets. It indicated a vulnerability to outflows. It also showed just how fat the Irish banks had become on less reliable sources of overseas money. The markets were looking into the future and asking how much more the Irish banks would have to pay for deposits. This implied the banks might struggle to achieve sustainable margins and, therefore, to be profitable.

I did not see how we could remain silent on this issue. We required a clear story about how the Irish banks would become profitable. Confidence in profitable banks is always fragile, but there is even less confidence in loss-making banks. Capital, liquidity and profitability were all needed to boost confidence in individual banks. They were also needed to show how a demonstrably viable banking system might emerge. Investors would find this proposition more compelling if we found it compelling ourselves. There was little point in building a well-capitalised but unprofitable banking system. Nor was there much to be said for hoping it might start lending into an economy which was not, at that time, demanding credit. We needed to tell a convincing story about the future of the banking system, not just point to a large dollop of capital and expect people to grasp its significance or to find it convincing.

Working back from the 31 March 2011 deadline, we started to identify what needed to be done, by when and who would lead each element. The centrepiece was the stress test. This was, again, to be called the Prudential Capital Assessment Review (PCAR). We all knew this would be our third attempt to establish the depth of losses in the banking system. This figure had proved elusive for over two years. For this reason, any estimate was likely to be treated with some scepticism. But we could address these doubts in a couple of ways. Toughening the economic scenarios was one. Increasing the target capital requirements was another. Both would result in larger capital demands for the banks, and this would give the exercise additional credibility.

But neither of these measures could improve the quality of the assets on which the capital calculations were going to be based. The banks were desperate to polish the asset turd, but this was self-defeating as everyone knew this is what they were doing. We had to get to the bottom of the problems in the loan books to extinguish doubts about the scale of losses. The answer was an initiative we called the Asset Quality Review (AQR).

The AQR was necessary because no one was satisfied with the existing loan loss estimates, nor were they confident the banks understood their own numbers. Although this had the potential to be a double-sided blade, such was the uncertainty about loans in the Irish banking system that a definitive assessment was attractive. In the previous stress tests, loan loss estimates had depended largely on the application of top-down scenarios to some reasonably high-level assumptions about the performance of different loan cohorts. By contrast, the process of transferring loans to NAMA relied on bottom-up estimates. Because the discounts NAMA made to these loans was so steep, some feared the same thing would happen if we took a loan-by-loan approach in the AQR.

This concern did not take enough account of the fact that NAMA was taking the very worst of the loans. Nor did it attach enough weight to the idiosyncrasies of NAMA. Clearly a loan-by-loan evaluation might, like trying to tidy a teenager's bedroom, throw-up some nasty surprises which might be better left unrevealed. But this was the point: by late 2010 there was nothing to be gained, and much credibility to be lost, by sweeping the realities of Irish banking under a carpet. The AQR had the potential to reduce the doubts about the banks' balance sheets. It also had the potential to remove uncertainty about the Irish authorities' willingness or competence to address these doubts. For both of these reasons, it was the right thing to do.

We sat around the table in Matthew's office to discuss our recommendations for the final design of the Financial Measures Programme. Everyone enjoyed these meetings, especially when Patrick was in an impish mood. If he was talkative at the beginning, this was the surest sign he was relaxed. But it was also a feint, if an unconscious one, since he could draw the unsuspecting into giving answers before they had processed his question. He did not set out to run tutorials, but meetings often ended up following the rules of an academic exchange.

On this occasion, he focused on the Asset Quality Review. He believed that uncertainty about the path of loan losses was the major vulnerability to the stress test. This was not just an issue of asset prices, which were still falling, it was about the quality of the underlying loans. Lending standards had been debased to such an extent that major questions existed about whether, in some cases, security for loans even existed.

I spent time in 2012 reviewing loan files. As well as being the best way to understand the quality of loans, it was a fascinating insight into Irish economic and social history. I saw plenty of examples of loans which, although recorded as development opportunities, never came to anything. They remained fields in rural Ireland, often miles from anywhere. There were also doubts about the legal enforceability of agreements stuck between borrowers and lenders in the 2000s. In some cases, it was unclear whether security for loans even existed. Even where security existed, and a loan had value, it was far from certain whether a bank could recover the asset. Such had been the scale of lending, that Irish banks owned all sorts of assets, from bogland in the Midlands to speculative overseas development plots. These assets had been on the banks' balance sheets for years. But such had been the pace of loan issuance that no one was confident in their value.

The AQR was our way to get a better fix on the prevalence of such problem loans. The problem was that we had only four months to do so. Patrick was adamant we had to find a third party to support the AQR. He wanted someone with a credible brand who would stand publicly behind its findings and, by extension, the Central Bank's recommendations. He suggested BlackRock, and it was not hard to understand why. It was one of the few financial institutions to have emerged with credit from the crisis. Its Chief Executive, Larry Fink, was well-respected, and it had a team in London with experience of similar assignments.

The AQR was proof of the adage that one should think carefully about whether to ask a question if one is wary of the answer. We needed to know what was really on the banks' books. BlackRock was the right partner to help us to do so. But the giant American firm needed to be managed. Precisely because it was staking its own reputation on the AQR, there was every incentive for it to err on the side of caution. Even a little caution might result in a large bill for the Irish taxpayer.

The banks were not keen to have their loan books forensically examined in case it required them to find yet more capital. The one with most to lose from the stress test and AQR was the one in the strongest position, Bank of Ireland. It had entered the crisis as the healthiest of a sickly group of banks. Because it had a fighting chance of raising private capital, and thereby avoiding majority public ownership, it did not want this next stress test to throw its plans off course. With the indefatigable Richie Boucher at the helm, Bank of Ireland was alone in having a credible story about its future viability. Boucher poured his energies into finding private investors for his bank. The last thing he needed was further pressure to raise more capital. He therefore mobilised his own team, under the equally impressive Andrew Keating, the bank's finance chief, to make sure the BlackRock exercise did not jeopardise his plans.

This made Bank of Ireland the easiest to deal with when we made requests for data for the AQR. Not only did it respond quickly, it provided better quality information than the other banks. This told its own story about Boucher's leadership. But it also pointed at a broader set of truths about the other banks. During the Celtic Tiger years, AIB, Anglo Irish Bank, Irish Nationwide and Bank of Ireland had jostled for top spot in the banking league table. By 2010, two of these four institutions no longer existed, in any recognisable sense, as banks. The third, AIB, had lost its way.

Unlike its remaining rival, Bank of Ireland, by late 2010 AIB was state-owned. Not that this was evident when I visited its headquarters in Ballsbridge. Although only Anglo Irish and Irish Nationwide had fallen further than AIB, there was a palpable sense of entitlement at the bank. It felt purposeless and lacked the sort of leadership Boucher was providing at Bank of Ireland. David Duffy's arrival as CEO did little to change the situation, or for that matter the bank's humility.

There was no such complacency at PTSB, the third bank to survive. It had emerged from a demerger with its parent, Irish Life. If AIB believed it was destined to survive no matter what, the smaller institution knew it had a fight on its hands. Its loan-to-deposit ratio was the highest of the major banks. Its balance sheet contained a portfolio of tracker mortgages which became increasingly unprofitable as interest rates fell. PTSB also lacked the scale of Bank of Ireland and AIB, affecting its ability to compete in what is a scale business. For these reasons, it was the one bank which flashed red in our work on viability.

Barclays Capital accelerated our analysis of these viability issues. We selected it to advise us on our options for individual banks and the banking system as a whole. Its team had flown to Dublin on a Saturday to pitch for this advisory role. The sharply dressed, youthful team buzzed with energy and ideas. Its leader, Ben Davey, immediately came across as engaging and astute. There was little of the swagger or abrasiveness typical of investment bankers. As he made the case for the appointment of his team, Davey moved with ease between his well-researched analysis of the banks, and his equally convincing assessment of the Irish banking system as a whole. He grasped that the ECB held the answers on funding, and that it was therefore pivotal to restoring confidence in the banks. In the coming months, we had many conversations about how we might enlist the ECB's support for a plan which served its own interests.

Davey was quick to articulate a story about the system which might be convincing to investors. His team had run the numbers, and it had concluded that as long as there was an assurance of continued funding from the ECB, there were options. He was adamant that the answer was not a rapid deleveraging. Not only would this absorb precious capital, it would destroy value. Given the support the State had already provided to the banks, this would be a bad outcome for taxpayers twice over.

Barclays had also looked at the pool of domestic deposits available to fund the banks. This confirmed that Ireland was heavily over-banked, and that this could only have one consequence for margins already under pressure in a world of low interest rates. This work confirmed my own belief that we had to tackle the question of viability head-on. We had to be able to tell a completely different story about the Irish banking system.

The job of compiling the final presentation fell to a team at the Central Bank and Boston Consulting Group (BCG). Afonso Nascimento, Portuguese by birth, led the BCG team. We were lucky to have him. The thoughtful consultant should, by rights, have been in Lisbon, fixing the crisis in his own country. He applied himself with such dedication that most of us forgot he was a consultant. I increasingly leaned on his judgement of people and issues, especially during those weeks when the workload came close to overwhelming us.

As we approached Christmas, the list of demands was piling up as surely as the snow which was falling on the city. One of the coldest winters in living memory had embraced Ireland, turning Dublin's streets into ice rinks, making a mess of the traffic and grounding flights. This rare meteorological event was a fitting metaphor for Ireland's situation, but in an oblique way. Under its covering of snow, Dublin looked like a different, changed place. By the end of the year, we knew that if we could rise to the occasion, the outlook for Ireland could look different in 2011. This was our challenge, as it was our opportunity.

Lesson #9: Know thyself. The importance of mental and physical wellbeing.

'Home at 2145. Pretty tired. Walked the dog. Difficult getting to sleep as reflections on recent days in the head.'

This is the final entry to my journal on 19 November 2010. Only the day before, Patrick Honohan had announced the bailout on national radio. It was a frenetic, restless period.

As I have re-read the journal I kept at that time, I have been reminded how much time we spent in back-to-back meetings. How little opportunity there was to escape from those intense discussions. Such was the pace of events that it was possible to spend entire days cocooned, usually discussing, with ever increasing intensity, a very limited range of subjects.

I look back now on the person I was ten years ago and realise three things. How poorly I understood the emotional and physical pressures I (and others) were experiencing. That my first response to these pressures was, in undiluted Alpha male mode, to tough them out. And, finally, that such limited self-care as I practiced was instinctual and reactive, not considered or planned.

This caught up with me almost immediately, and completely unexpectedly, after we completed the March 2011 stress test. It had been one of many remarkable events in a remarkable year in Ireland. The election of a new government after years of Fianna Fáil dominance. The weeklong Royal visit. President Obama's twenty-four hours in Ireland. All of these events grabbed the public's attention. But a baby gorilla, born in captivity at Dublin Zoo, captured the public's heart.

It had been a talking point at my daughters' school, so a few days after we published the stress test results, I took them to the Phoenix Park. It was raining and the zoo was quiet. A small group had gathered at the gorilla enclosure. Here were two groups of primates watching one another through a transparent Perspex divide. As I moved towards the enclosure, there was an audible gasp as the mother appeared with the recently born youngster locked to her back. I pointed this out to my daughters. They stood transfixed. There was no tugging at my sleeve, no pleading to see other animals. It was a remarkable encounter, and we stood perfectly still as if in a trance.

It was not until I turned away from the enclosure that something else had happened to me. For months, I had a singular focus, one channel for my physical and emotional energy, one preoccupation for my mind. The Financial Measures Programme was not the main thing in my life for a time, it was the only thing. It excluded more or less everything else. It became more than a task, it became an obsession. And at that moment, standing in front of the gorilla enclosure, it suddenly felt as if the resulting adrenaline drained from my system. As it did so, I suddenly felt empty, like I had suffered a loss, and was now without a purpose.

I was grieving. I just did not know it at the time. I have since seen others experiencing similar emotions in their careers, particularly when they have had to leave high-status, high-pressure roles. This is not surprising as work gives purpose to our lives. It defines who we are in our own minds, and in the eyes of others. But we tend to downplay the effects of these endings in our working lives, as we often fail to see the emotional consequences.

❆   ❆   ❆

I watched those at the centre of the COVID-19 outbreak and sought to understand the emotions they were experiencing. Because the pandemic has been a life or death struggle, and its knock-on effects so widespread, there is no question in my mind that the pressures have been of a different magnitude to those I witnessed during the global financial crisis. The sobering deaths of medical practitioners were a stark reminder that crisis management in a pandemic has a very different meaning. The increasingly ashen and drawn faces of the politicians and officials on the frontline told its own story too. The weight of responsibility aged people in front of our eyes. And these were the effects we could observe. The consequences of stress are not always apparent, and mental health issues can take a hidden toll. In this regard, we will only understand the true effects of the pandemic in years to come. And because the pandemic has touched everyone, these effects may well be widespread.

For those at the centre of events, and therefore in the public eye, these pressures are even greater. And they are unavoidable. Public scrutiny is an inevitable consequence of public office, but it is hard to appreciate the nature and intensity of its effects from a distance. Knowing that one is doing the right thing can be sustaining, but the words of a critic will still sting. I can recall more than a few occasions when very senior Irish officials took exception to something a journalist or commentator had written. For those involved in a crisis, it is always a very personal experience. And even where a professional mask obscures the effects of criticism, there is nonetheless pain on the wearer's face.

A crisis is always a formative, demanding experience. And however battle hardened, however robust, someone might appear to be, everyone survives on reserves of energy and sleep which run down quickly in high pressure situations. And everyone suffers from the consequences of these depleting reserves. One of these consequences is being unable to see that the reserves are running low. Another is to resist this conclusion. The effect in either case is the same: we become less effective.

Caring for oneself is therefore a necessary part of crisis management. What this means in practice depends entirely on the needs of an individual. It does not mean a rigid adherence to rules on diet, sleep and exercise. These things are important, but they are baseline conditions for wellbeing. For some people, a long, intoxicated evening in a nightclub, surrounded by people, may be the right answer. For others, it could be that a weekend somewhere remote, away from other humans, provides the solution. I have found that whisky, walking the dog and escaping into the world of P.G. Wodehouse all work for me, but good luck getting that advice from a doctor.

A crisis is one way of discovering what works, but it is not a low risk one, not least because you might leave it too late. There are ways to prepare. One of them is to improve your self-knowledge. This can be fun as well as enlightening. And if it reveals that being in chaotic, high-pressure decision-making roles are not your thing, it will have been money well spent. Such a process is also a good way, during or after a crisis, to make sense of your experiences. I certainly learned a lot about myself when, with the help of a psychologist, I went back over my experiences in Ireland. Writing this book has also been therapeutic.

We are a multitude of qualities, some strengths, others weaknesses, and a crisis reveals those traits in glorious Technicolour. It has been intriguing to watch how different personalities have handled themselves in the COVID-19 crisis. It has confirmed my impression that individuals with a greater capacity for introspection, with an inner voice (see Lesson #7), tend to handle a crisis better, and they emerge from it as stronger, fuller human beings. But this is hardly surprising. Where someone has an intrinsic motivation, or feels called to a higher purpose, they are more likely to find the resources to sustain themselves and others. I have no doubt that determination, grit and stamina are qualities which help in a crisis. But bloody-mindedness has its limits, especially when not accompanied by an equivalent ability to stand back and refresh one's judgements. Hanging in there for its own sake is a form of survival. It is not a platform for leadership.

A key, if overlooked indicator, of an individual's suitability for a crisis is whether they are going to enjoy the experience. Doubtless there are some who would balk at the idea that a crisis might be enjoyed. How could this be so, they might reasonably ask, when people are losing loved ones, experiencing hardship or being made unemployed? But this critique misses some important truths about human motivation. No one should enjoy the *consequences* of a crisis. There is, however, immense personal satisfaction to be found in the enjoyment of its *resolution*. I certainly did not enjoy every moment of the Irish crisis. But I enjoyed more than enough of it because I knew I was doing something which mattered. I also enjoyed the conflict, the struggle, the difficulties, the camaraderie and the humorous moments along the way. This did not mean I was not serious, nor did it mean the responsibilities weighed less on my shoulders. But it did tell me that I was in the right place, at the right time and, for the most part, doing the right things for their own sake.

And on those few occasions when I stepped away from the melee, I felt better in myself and saw things more clearly. I have a very distinct memory of a walk with my father on a cold, crisp morning in February 2011, during the course of which I sorted out a few issues in my head which had been bothering me. The combination of familiar company and hopeful winter sunlight cleared my mind. And as we moved on foot through the frost-covered countryside, I moved to a place of greater peace and clarity. Walking and crisis management go hand in hand.

In the coming years, we will learn how those most involved in the pandemic found ways to cope. Common to all of these stories will be references to people, places, objects or experiences on which they could rely. These 'secure bases' are the places where we find consolation and renewal. They are as sustaining in a crisis as they are nourishing in life. We therefore need to comprehend what they are, and we need to know how to access them. This requires that we understand ourselves, if not perfectly, then at least well enough to be able to know where to turn when the pressure comes on. A crisis tests us in ways we cannot anticipate, and as we are examined, our resources deplete as each hour passes. Leaders, with noble intentions, often put themselves to the bottom of the list of priorities. This can lead to a form of self-defeating martyrdom. It is much better to know how we ourselves cope, put it into practice, and then help others to do the same.

Some lessons for leaders in a crisis:

1. **Keep a journal to provide perspective.** There will be many moments during a crisis when you feel overwhelmed. Fatigue may amplify the effects, and it is easy to lose perspective. Keeping a record not only allows you to track events over time, but a conscious process of sitting down and writing enables the exploration of those emotions, which in the moment, may feel insurmountable.

2. **Your physical and mental health matter more than you realise**. The first person you are likely to lose sight of in a crisis is yourself. You are unlikely to realise it has happened. Like a lobster growing drowsy in warming

water, you will not see yourself becoming tired, physically drained nor increasingly short tempered. But others will. They will see how it impacts your performance, and your condition will impact their performance. The less you diverge from your normal habits or routine, the more likely you are to be able to manage yourself through a crisis.

3. **Introverts need to take extra care in a crisis.** A crisis not only speeds up working life, it intensifies the experience. This places significant demands on everyone involved. But it is especially stretching for people who find it more difficult to spend long periods of time in large groups. As it is for those who value time to reflect away from others. It is the leader's responsibility to make sure that everyone can have some breathing space, but particularly those who need it most.

10.

Taking a Punt

Not long after we completed the second stress test in March 2011, Dwayne Price and I were invited to Athens to advise the Bank of Greece on its own Troika-backed stress test. We flew to the Greek capital via London, landing late at night. The Central Bank sent a car to collect us. It was pleasantly warm. The route took us past the university where there had been some unrest in recent months. Riot policemen lined the road which runs alongside the campus. In the city centre, we could see roadblocks and fences. There were flashing lights and the wail of sirens. It felt like a place on the edge of a revolution, or at least a place organising to prevent one.

The bracing Mediterranean sunshine woke me early the following morning. I decided to walk from the hotel to the Bank of Greece. The route would take me past Syntagma Square, home to the Greek government and parliament. I was keen to see for myself whether the reports of large crowds of protesters were accurate.

It was hot and before long I was uncomfortable in my suit. I paused and removed my jacket next to a group of armed policemen, their expressions hidden behind sunglasses. As I got closer to Syntagma Square, I heard the noise of drums and horns. Walking on I could see people gathered in the shadow of the parliament building. They were holding placards and flags. Then I heard some loud bangs. I assumed fireworks were being let off. Only when I saw people running away from me did I realise that something was going on. Turning a corner, I saw another line of policemen. There was lots of smoke in front of them. People were holding items of clothing to their faces. It was obviously tear gas. I turned, hoping to find a route which might take me away from the enveloping cloud. When I arrived a few minutes later at the Bank of Greece, I noticed my eyes were stinging and moist. This felt like a proper crisis. It was exhilarating.

An Garda Síochána made a show of force, in its own distinct way, twice in Dublin when I was working in the city. The first was during Queen Elizabeth's visit. The second during Barack Obama's brief layover. There was next to no trouble on either occasion. Throughout the crisis, Dublin, unlike Athens, remained peaceful and safe. The Troika moved around the city freely. Irish officials and politicians were able to do the same. They faced conditions identical to those private citizens enjoyed. Other than the odd intrusion from a cameraman, I don't recall anyone from the Troika ever saying they felt threatened or unsafe. A group of bankers was hassled once while waiting to enter Dame Street, but this is likely to have owed more to the proximity of the pubs in Temple Bar.

It was on one of these journeys that I saw Patrick Honohan at his brilliant best. We had been at a meeting of the Department of Finance together and had decided to walk to Dame Street once it finished. It was a chilly day and Patrick was in his trademark Macintosh.

As we walked down Trinity Street, a woman, about sixty years old, approached Patrick. She had spotted the Governor and broken away from a small group of anorak-clad protestors. 'Professor Honohan, Professor Honohan,' she began.

Patrick kept straight on, easing his deceptively demanding pace only a fraction. 'Hello,' he replied jovially, inviting her to address him.

'Professor Honohan, is it true we are going to get the Irish pound back?'

There were no journalists present. We were some distance from her fellow protestors. On the face of it, she was an ordinary citizen asking a question then being widely discussed. Even so, anything Patrick might have said would be open to interpretation, something he knew only too well. And even if she was not carrying secret recording equipment, she might have reported his response to her group. Time stood still for a few moments.

Central bank governors measure their words carefully. Great significance is attached to their most mundane or insignificant utterances. For these reasons, most tend not to say a great deal. When they do say something, it is often deliberately opaque or oblique, and it is generally always scripted.

Patrick was not a career central banker and not of this mould. Nor was he temperamentally inclined to curb his natural candour. So this encounter had the potential to be problematic. We were in the middle of a crisis, and there was growing speculation about Ireland's continued membership of the euro. The risks of any response were high, but it was not in Patrick's nature to avoid a good question asked politely.

Doubtless these dangers flashed through Patrick's mind as he weighed his response.

He stopped walking. He paused. He looked her straight in the eyes. 'Oh, that's very interesting. What colour do you think it should be? Pink? Blue?'

She laughed, obviously delighted at this example of his famous wit, and walked back to her companions. We continued our journey and passed through the Central Bank's entrance. He had navigated this potential flashpoint with aplomb.

Patrick's reply said much for his speed of thought, humour and his ability to treat everyone as he found them. It also spoke to his accessibility. Most central bank governors would have been safely cocooned in the rear seats of a car. If they had been on their feet, a security official or press officer would have intervened to prevent the questioner or divert the question. But this is not how he wanted to live his life as governor. This said much about him as an individual. It also said much about his essential Irishness.

The Irish were not, in 2010, inclined to consider Irishness as an unquestionable good. The crisis had triggered, or perhaps reawakened, an appetite for self-criticism and mortification. The national media was awash with denunciations of the country by its own citizens. The origins of the crisis were, of course, in many ways very Irish. The obsession with land and property. An unhealthy attachment to informal relationships in business and government. But under Patrick's leadership, the recovery was proving to be very Irish too, and in some very good ways. An openness to outsiders, personal warmth in relationships with the Troika's officials, and humour in the face of adversity.

And Patrick's insistence on speaking openly and honestly about the country's condition. Had it been otherwise, I doubt the nation would have come to trust Patrick in the way it did. He did not go in for flannel, preferring straightforward language. He did not talk down to people. He appeared to describe things as they were. Our encounter outside the Central Bank neatly encapsulated his approach, and it said something very reassuring about the health of Irish democracy and freedom, and therefore about Ireland.

Except he did not answer the question. He deflected the woman's enquiry with a question of his own. In doing so he avoided being drawn into a discussion he did not want to have with anyone at that time. The woman did not know that her question was already on his mind. Such were the country's debts that there were serious doubts about its sustainability.

The Troika's arrival did not solve this problem. In fact, it was likely to make it worse as Ireland was going to have to borrow more. For these reasons, the governor was forced to weigh whether an exit from the euro might be necessary to relieve the Irish State from a potentially crippling debt burden. He did not want to have to address this question. He certainly did not like to have to think about the serious, and very damaging, consequences of leaving the euro. But he knew it fell to him to ask whether Ireland could afford the costs of remaining in the currency union.

The Irish people were threatened with a massive debt burden. One that could endure for three or four generations. The Department of Finance was responsible for day-to-day management of the public finances and had to work out what constituted an acceptable level of debt. The key word was 'acceptable'. It could be defined in a number of ways, some objective, some subjective. To do so required answers to a number of questions. What would constitute a sustainable debt burden? How much should Ireland pay for this debt? Over what period of time? This analysis required a number of assumptions to be made about the economy's future performance. But even the strongest economy could only support a certain amount of debt.

But what options were available if ministers concluded that the debt burden was too great? There were several, ranging from continued negotiation with the Troika, in the hope of a better deal, to default. The government had options. Ireland remained a high income country, and there was a stock of private wealth, so taxes could be raised. There was scope to cut public expenditure further. On paper at least, austerity could continue, and on paper Ireland could borrow more.

But societies do not operate on paper. The ever more aggressive pursuit of austerity could, some feared, endanger the country's social fabric. Unemployment was high, and young people were again emigrating for work. The levels of personal indebtedness were high by international standards. But where did this leave a country without its own currency, no direct control of monetary policy and with few fiscal choices?

When journalists and commentators started to question the affordability of the debt, and by extension euro membership, the official response was curt. Ireland's politicians studiously avoided talking about the country's membership of the euro. It was no more up for debate than the location of the Cliffs of Moher. Or so it might have seemed from the outside. The Troika's arrival had created breathing space, but it had not changed the fundamental indebtedness equation. And Ireland's politicians knew it was a finely balanced one.

The close relationship of Ireland's politicians to voters, and the system of multi-member constituencies, are sometimes identified as sources of parochialism in national politics. It struck me as a source of strength during the crisis. Not only did it allow politicians to track the attitudes of voters, it served as a safety valve at a time of anxiety and hardship. It was therefore fundamentally democratic at a time when an unelected organisation, the Troika, had significant power in the country. As no one from Frankfurt or Brussels was drinking with voters in the pubs of Limerick, Cork or Letterkenny, or attending funerals in Athlone, Waterford or Dundalk, it could not be said they had a finger on the pulse of Irish public opinion. The signals the politicians were picking up from voters suggested an acceptance of the government's tough measures. But as one politician put it to me, this did not imply a limitless appetite for economic hardship, especially among those with nothing further to lose. In such a small country, the crisis touched everyone, directly or indirectly. The prospect of it getting harder was unattractive, not least to politicians seeking re-election.

Such were the difficulties facing the economy, and such was the burden of debt, that the alternative of default had to be considered. Options were therefore developed for a future in which Ireland found itself outside the euro. This work was a closely guarded secret. While not quite the stuff of spy fiction, there was more than a whiff of the cloak and dagger about Project Greenfield. Its existence was not acknowledged, and material was shared on a need to know basis. These were the sort of precautions the Financial Services Authority used to handle highly sensitive intelligence.

Such secrecy was necessary as redenomination would be a messy and difficult process. It would lead to very significant losses for Irish depositors and the ECB. Banks would need time to translate euro balances into the new currency, and the Central Bank's currency centre at Sandyford would need time to produce new notes and coins. Time would also be needed to move cash to branches and ATMs across Ireland. This would have required a long, and very dramatic, bank holiday weekend.

The media inevitably focused on physical cash as its interest in the issue increased. Articles about the design, production and distribution of notes and coins simplified an otherwise complicated issue. It made abstract ideas comprehensible. But largely missing from this coverage was the obvious, if uncomfortable, truth of redenomination: that a new currency would be worth less than the euro. And this was the whole point. The State needed to reduce its euro liabilities, and to do so it had to relinquish the euro.

This was an incredibly sobering prospect. But what would the reaction have been if Irish people had woken up to bank balances denominated in Irish pounds? The Irish Pound had seen plenty of ups and downs before the euro replaced it in 1999. There had been currency and capital controls on several occasions following the Second World War. But there was no precedent for a withdrawal from the euro area, and it would have been an extreme event, with potentially very serious consequences for Ireland.

And the issue had to be evaluated in these terms. Greece, Ireland and Portugal may have felt at times as if they were trapped in a high security prison. But this was only the beginning of their difficulties. An escape attempt would be perilous. Ireland could create a breach in the currency union walls, but it then had to survive in a world where its creditors would, to put it mildly, be deeply disenchanted with Dublin. They might demand settlement of their debts in euros, which would leave Dublin no better off unless it could cut a deal. The euro area might impose sanctions to deter others tempted to flee. The EU might, in a show of force, eject Ireland from the Single Market. None of this looked attractive.

But how close did Ireland come to exiting the euro? The answer is that it never came very close, but it did come closer than most Irish citizens might realise. Unlike the Greek government, the Irish government never played the redenomination card in private or public. In one respect, it was not very Irish to do so. But it also reflected a sensible assessment of the risks of discussing redenomination. Any conversations on the subject risked being exposed in a city not known for its habit of keeping secrets. Even the most circumspect Irish official was a target for foreign intelligence services. I have little doubt that Ireland's EU partners kept tabs on decisions taken in Dublin. I considered it prudent to assume my own phone calls were at risk of being overheard. Kevin Cardiff and Patrick Honohan were prime targets. There was a lot of money at stake, and countries work hard to protect their own interests. Ireland had the potential to threaten these interests.

By evaluating the alternatives to euro membership, the Irish authorities at least signalled some resistance to agreeing an open-ended financial commitment. The Troika held most of the cards, but it did not hold all of them. It was right to look at what could be done in the event that either the Troika failed to agree a fair settlement, or the government decided enough was enough. But no one wanted to break with Europe. Redenomination was never seen as a serious or attractive alternative to a future in Europe. As the new government was soon to discover, there was something worse than breaking an election promise not to put more money into the banks.

Lesson #10: Confidence is not competence.
The uses of doubt.

In the spellbinding film *Free Solo*, the climber, Alex Honnold, is shown making an attempt to free climb El Capitan in Yosemite National Park. The risks of the ascent have been explained to us by this point in the documentary. Even a non-climber can grasp the difficulty of the endeavour. From a purely mountaineering perspective, it was a highly technical and demanding challenge.

But this is only one dimension of the task Honnold faces. In an intriguing subplot, the production team explains the moral dilemma of filming the climb. They acknowledge that their mere presence might put pressure on Honnold to take more risks than if he were unobserved. As they talk about these issues, we begin to understand the added psychological pressures of climbing while being filmed. And not just observed: caught on camera in the making of a major motion picture.

So when Honnold pulls out because he is not confident about a particular manoeuvre, not only do we witness someone acknowledging his limits as a climber. We observe an individual able to put the psychological pressures of performance to one side. We know what he knows: that he might be tempted, because he is being filmed, to push himself too far, to do something with which, as a climber, he is not comfortable. Not only is it an incredible example of mountaineering risk management, it is an inspiring example of self-awareness and self-control.

It is also a brilliant example of decision-making under pressure. For Honnold, a crisis was never more than one failed hold away, one slip. This uncertainty powers the narrative. But the struggle on the mountain is not the only story. The battle within the climber's own mind holds our attention. The experience of his extreme endeavour might not be universal, but the doubt, uncertainty and falling confidence are all emotions to which we can relate.

I was never completely confident about what I was doing during the Irish crisis. At certain moments, I felt less sure about things and took myself away to understand why. At other times, when I sensed I was being too confident, I did the same thing. I never doubted my ability to do the job. But I did doubt whether I was doing it in the right way. And I also questioned, out of habit as much as anything else, whether I was doing the right things.

Doubt comes in many forms. Some of its manifestations are useful in a crisis, while others are disabling. The distinction exists in the nature of the doubt. There is a big difference between doubts which arise about *why* one is doing something, and doubts which emerge about *how* one is doing it. I never questioned why the work mattered. This struck me as self-evident. Only when we had reached the end of the programme did I start to think my reasons to be there might have changed.

I saw it as my job to be confident in my role. Not to put on a brave face, and certainly not to appear too sure, but to project calm and a sense of purpose, particularly during the more challenging moments. In private, or with my closest colleagues, I gave myself permission to explore my own questions about how we were approaching issues. I was fortunate that Patrick and Matthew, both natural reflectors, were happy to have these conversations, not least as it helped their own thought processes. I was also fortunate in being able to talk, often at length, with my good friend, Gareth Davis, recently returned to Ireland after a successful career in the US. As well as having a first rate mind, Gareth also had a different, and very original, perspective on where Ireland found itself and what it could do next.

One challenge in a crisis is to find time to think and therefore explore the doubts one may be having. Another is to be able to do so in a way which does not spook colleagues. Perhaps the biggest challenge is to work out what one should have doubts about. When there is much going on, and things are moving at a pace, our antenna can be overwhelmed. Working out what matters, and what does not, is a perennial challenge for executives.

Business schools do not teach doubt, and there are few management books which talk about its inevitability. If anything, the opposite is true, with emphasis placed instead on the importance of bold and purposeful leadership. In a complex, uncertain and non-linear world, the standard model of leadership seems terribly outdated. I am not sure how it is possible to lead unless one has understood where one is going. Doubt helps us to make this determination.

I used to conclude meetings by asking if anyone had any questions or doubts. I thought that by asking this I was being inclusive. I can now see it was the wrong question. Everyone has doubts, most of the time. And a meeting is a poor place to ask people what they are feeling or experiencing. It would have been much better to ask for help, for when a leader says they are unsure of something and asks for help, it engages and energises the team.

❄   ❄   ❄

The COVID-19 pandemic will provide many case studies about the role of doubt in leadership and policy making during a crisis. As the outbreak developed, pressure built on politicians and public health officials to provide solutions, and to be *seen* to provide solutions. This is a normal reaction after a crisis, disaster or other major event, and it creates the conditions in which poor decisions are more likely to be made. In the heat of the moment, the aphorism 'act in haste, repent at leisure' is often forgotten.

To take one specific example from the pandemic, it would have been easy, and possibly attractive, for more governments looking for confidence boosting gestures to have required the wearing of protective face masks in public. Fortunately, doubts were raised about the impact of this policy on the supply to medical professionals. Similarly, doubts were raised about the side effects of face masks. What if people touched their masks when the virus was present? What if mask wearing made people less likely to ignore social distancing rules? What if it made them more confident to travel and therefore more likely to spread the virus? Because the merits of these and other ideas were debated, better decisions were made.

The very nature of the virus was a challenge to our instinctive desire for certainty and security. There was no known cure. Nor was it clear which, if any, treatments worked. Very few governments had a reliable picture of how many citizens had contracted the virus, and there was confusion about which symptoms might reliably indicate the presence of the virus. The policy response was every bit as uncertain as it had been during the early phases of the global financial crisis. But as in that earlier crisis, politicians and officials who acknowledged these doubts, and explained that their actions were designed accordingly, seem to have been trusted more. Conversely, when everyone can see that things are highly uncertain, the leader who appeared inoculated to doubt, or in denial, only added to our concerns. There was already enough unease without politicians adding more through poorly judged, bullish interventions, or urging people to experiment with household cleaning products.

Doubt will serve us well as we look for lasting solutions to the public health and economic effects of the disease. There will be an inevitable, and healthy, tension between public health professionals and politicians. The former will argue that we ought to go further in some areas of disease prevention and healthcare provision. The politicians, conscious of the wider implications for individual liberty, economic well-being and government finances, will resist. It is precisely the same tension which existed between regulators and politicians following the financial crisis. The banking system could have been made even safer, but it would have come at a cost. Doubt helped us to explore those policy choices after 2008. It will help us in the 2020s as we grapple with the fallout of the COVID-19 pandemic, and we begin the work of making our societies more resilient.

Some lessons for leaders in a crisis:

1. **You will make mistakes. Learn from them.** Learning to do something to a high standard requires a process of trial and error. Becoming competent at something takes time. It also requires constant questioning of one's reasons for beginning the journey, of how well one is progressing, and of what one has learned on the way. Doubt can help you become more competent.

2. **There will be a reason something does not feel right**. Although we are emotional beings, we tend to downplay this truth about ourselves when in a professional setting. We believe that, in work, analytical, left-brain responses are better than emotional, right-brain ones. But a doubt is something felt first and explored intellectually later. As emotions and instincts have something important to say, heeding your feelings in a crisis is important, as is giving yourself time to explore them.

3. **Find a structured way to surface doubts, but in a different setting**. Most of us are able to see doubt and hesitation in the faces of others, even when they have not said a word. If a leader fails to acknowledge these feelings, problems can build up and people can feel disenfranchised. But it is rarely productive to surface these doubts in formal meetings. Creating a safe space where people can talk openly about what is on their minds is an essential task of leadership, and not only in a crisis.

11.

How Much?

The new cabinet sat around a rectangular table in Government Buildings. Their heads were down. It did not look like a group who had just won an election. Perhaps this was to be expected. We had just finished our presentation about how much it was likely to cost to fix the banks. I could feel the tension increasing in the room. Everyone was waiting for someone else to say something. Labour Party Minister Joan Burton, unable to restrain herself, spoke first.

'We're not going to give the banks that much money. It would be political suicide.'

We were there to explain the reality of the banks to the new cabinet. I am sure all they could hear, once we gave our estimates, was a future newspaper headline: 'New government agrees largest bank bailout to date.' The sober atmosphere in that gathering nicely illustrated a problem of democratic politics: once a government is elected it has to break promises made on the campaign.

It also illustrated the challenge facing the Labour Party. It had gone to the polls arguing strongly against further bank bailouts. Under threat from Sinn Féin on the left of Irish politics, its stance made political sense. But it was unrealistic. It was also incompatible with its support for euro membership, not to mention its full-throated commitment to the European project. Nonetheless, Joan Burton was correct about the implications for Labour. In the 2016 election it took a beating.

I looked to my left, where John Moran was sitting with Ben Davey from Barclays Capital who was advising the Central Bank. Neither said anything. John had engineered the briefing in the hope it would help the cabinet to accept the recommendations of the Financial Measures Programme. But it was not looking hopeful after we stopped talking. Labour's leader, Eamon Gilmore, reinforced Burton's comments. This prompted Taoiseach Enda Kenny's most important adviser, Andrew McDowell, to offer some pacifying remarks. Leo Varadkar asked about the competitive future of the banks, which gave John Moran his opening to explain why the banks needed to be restructured.

While all of this was going on, Michael Noonan sat and said nothing. The new Minister of Finance had perfected the art of keeping his own counsel. In a profession better known for noisy oratory than meditative inner dialogues, this distinguished him. But it was more than a mask. Over many decades in Irish politics, he had seen what worked, and what did not. He also had wisdom: he knew what he did not know.

A few weeks later, on the day we published the stress test, he would buy me a pint of Guinness in Reilly's Bar, the nearest pub to the Department of Finance. On that evening, he found himself surrounded by adoring younger women, the freshly minted saviour of Ireland and its banks.

In the ad hoc cabinet briefing, I had observed someone who knew how events were going to play out.

After the meeting broke up, John, Ben and I walked across the street to the Merrion Hotel. John was his normal ebullient self despite the desultory atmosphere in the room. He said he thought we had done enough to confront the new government with the realities of the banking situation. They needed time to digest what governing in a Troika process was going to mean in practice. He said some reaction from Labour was predictable given its messages on the campaign. He called Andrew McDowell, and McDowell confirmed John's analysis. It was also important to remember, he stressed, that this was an informal session, not a formal cabinet meeting.

John had made himself busy before the election to understand what the new Fine Gael-led administration expected from the Central Bank. He knew Michael Noonan from Limerick, where the new Finance Minister's wife had been John's primary school teacher. John's research suggested that the new government wanted to deal with the banks early, and once only, as it would be politically damaging to do otherwise. The potential sticking point was the cost of a further bailout. It was highly unlikely the new government would oppose the Troika's demands, but its acceptance could not be assumed.

The timing of the informal cabinet session could not have been better as our work on the Financial Measures Programme was drawing to a conclusion. We were starting to get a better fix on the quality of the assets on the banks' balance sheets. We had developed some good ideas on how a smaller system might fund itself without central bank support. We had also been able to examine options for the ailing credit unions. Solutions for the most problematic assets – what came to be known as the NAMA 2 option – were considered. Different options for the defunct shells of Anglo and Irish Nationwide

Building Society were debated. The comprehensive view of how we might create a functioning system, which we had so desperately wanted for months, was coming together. And, for the first time, we had reliable data to support our emerging conclusions.

In a short space of time we had closed many of the gaps in our knowledge which had bedevilled the earlier stress test. We also had the resources, unlike in 2010, to do the exercise justice. But I continued to worry that people saw the stress test as the cure-all. The problems with the banking system went far beyond its stock of bad loans. Ireland's banks had outgrown Ireland, leaving a shortfall of deposits, not only capital, to be addressed.

Without action on funding, Ireland's banks would have found themselves indefinitely relying on central bank funding. They would also have had to pay well over the odds in private markets to attract deposits. This would have left the banking system structurally unprofitable, or at least insufficiently profitable to attract new private sector investors. This meant it had to shrink. Yet few wanted to hear this message.

We presented these arguments to the Central Bank's board one evening in early 2011. It had little practical influence on events by this point, but it needed to be kept on side if our more radical proposals were to make it as far as the final published recommendations. We had already described the shape of a restructured banking system to the Troika. The essence of this proposal was a new, slimmed down structure, with two 'pillar banks' at its core. Like a football manager describing different formations for his team, John Moran explained the pillar bank concept.

Bank of Ireland and AIB were to be the main domestic banks – the 'pillars'. Competition would come from those non-Irish banks still operating in Ireland, principally Ulster Bank and KBC. In this model, the sub-scale EBS would be pushed into AIB. PTSB, with its problematic loan book and high loan-to-deposit ratio, would be moved into a holding structure so its liabilities could be repaid over time.

There were a number of advantages to this proposal. It gave Bank of Ireland and AIB a fighting chance of survival in the private sector. It removed two weak banks, PTSB and EBS, from the system. And because it identified a path to viability for the system as a whole, it offered the prospect that not only would the State have to inject less capital, it might actually be able to sell down its existing stakes in the banks more quickly.

But were our Irish colleagues and the Troika ready for such a radical transformation? In his book, *Thinking, Fast and Slow*, the behavioural psychologist, Daniel Kahneman, describes a cognitive bias called anchoring. This occurs where an individual depends too heavily on an initial piece of information (the 'anchor') when making decisions. Once the value of this anchor is set, all future discussions occur, directly and indirectly, in reference to this anchor. We knew that the presentation was bold, but had it moved the anchor? Could we persuade people that the system with which they were familiar was, in fact, an unhelpful distortion?

It was not necessary to travel too far back in time to see that our proposed structure looked familiar. The rapid rise of Anglo Irish Bank, and the aggressive incursions of Ulster Bank and Halifax Bank of Scotland, had distorted a system which, for a long time, Bank of Ireland and AIB dominated.

This system had served Ireland well for many decades but, by 2011, it was unrecognisable, having become bloated on imported euros. It needed to learn to survive on a diet of domestic deposits. But continued Central Bank funding was necessary for this transition, and this meant we needed the ECB's support. As it could not countenance open-ended funding for banks, Irish or otherwise, the ECB needed a reason to continue its support while the banks sorted themselves out. Our plan provided this reason.

The problem we faced was the familiarity of the existing banking system. The Department of Finance and European Commission had expressed their initial reservations about the proposal before the board meeting. Kevin Cardiff sat on the Central Bank's board. He listened carefully to John's presentation. When John had finished, Kevin, with characteristic tact, noted that some of his colleagues in the department had questions about the plan. The truth was that the structural issues were dividing opinion within the Irish authorities. And it would soon become an area of open disagreement between Dame Street and Merrion Street.

As we moved nearer to the publication of the Financial Measures Programme, the Department of Finance's opposition hardened. It wanted to retain PTSB as a third pillar bank. It did not want AIB to subsume EBS. Neither argument was without merit. PTSB had the slimmest of chances of becoming a third force in the market, especially if Ulster Bank and KBC withdrew completely. AIB's absorption of EBS would be operationally challenging at a time when the larger bank was trying to sort itself out. But it was hard to see how two weak banks, PTSB and EBS, would contribute to a strong and viable banking system. In fact, there were many reasons to believe their continued existence might stand in its way.[1]

The credit unions provided a further flashpoint between the Central Bank and Department of Finance. This was also an issue of viability. The more experienced members of the IMF team had seen it all before. When a banking system grows too large, business is sucked from second tier institutions, such as credit unions or smaller mutuals, and they are left to survive on the crumbs.

This was more or less the situation facing many Irish credit unions in 2011. But it was only the beginning of their problems. Credit unions are sub-scale businesses. They perform an activity which requires scale, and it is therefore hard for them to compete. They struggle to generate capital, and they therefore struggle to invest. They are also more vulnerable to loan defaults as they have small, concentrated loan books. It is not impossible for credit unions to prosper, but it is difficult.

There was an opportunity in 2011 to put the sector on a more stable footing. This solution could have addressed the short-term solvency issues. It could have helped credit unions grow and develop. But here our good intentions ran into the sector's single largest, if self-created, problem: its main representative body, the Irish League of Credit Unions (ILCU).

I had been warned about ILCU before arriving in Dublin. I was a little sceptical of the claims made about its influence. I changed my mind quickly when I saw first-hand its influence at a Dáil Committee meeting in 2010. Although the League

---

[1] It is perhaps sufficient to observe, a decade later, that neither AIB nor PTSB have managed to escape government ownership. This did not have to be so.

was not asking the questions, it had planted them. It would have been a more honest process had ILCU employees, rather than the elected politicians, gathered around the horseshoe table in the committee room.

We tried to work with the ILCU to redesign the sector. We actively considered various combinations of credit unions. A 'hub and spoke' model seemed plausible, with benefits accruing to the smaller 'spoke' credit unions from using the systems and processes of a 'hub' credit union. This had the additional advantage of preserving the identity of individual credit unions, and the all-important common bond would have been retained. Members would have seen no difference when walking through the door of their local credit union. This well-intentioned work was designed to strengthen this small but important sector. Sadly, if predictably, the sector has since experienced a slow yet relentless decline. This could have been avoided. An opportunity was missed in 2011.

These debates continued into 2012. In the context of the Financial Measures Programme, the credit unions were a small issue. But the failure to grasp this nettle, combined with the reluctance to push through a comprehensive re-structuring of the banking system, demonstrated the limits to the Central Bank's authority. The Department of Finance had always kept a tight grip on financial sector policy, and it was not about to let go. But had we not pushed for change, I suspect very little would have happened.

But if we were treading water with the credit unions, we were growing more confident of meeting the end of March deadline for publication. This added to a broader feeling of optimism at that time. Bank of Ireland announced it had secured investment from US billionaire Wilbur Ross and

Fairfax Financial, a US investment house. The Central Bank started to receive calls from investors interested in Irish property assets. All we had to do was convince the outside world that we finally had answers to the many questions about Ireland's banks. How severe were the losses? How much would it cost to deal with them? Where would the money come from? By the beginning of March, we thought we had most of the answers.

Lesson #11: Crises end, but the causes endure.

It was hot and we wanted to get away from the crowds on the busy summer streets of Venice. I was with my wife and daughters. In the hope of finding some relief, we walked to the northern edge of the main island. Turning a corner, we suddenly felt a breeze from the lagoon. Feeling renewed and refreshed, we agreed to continue on foot to the train station. We turned west and crossed a bridge. But all of a sudden, as we took in the square ahead of us, we felt a sudden sadness.

We were, quite unexpectedly, in the Ghetto, that area of Venice which had long been the main home of the city's Jewish population. Soldiers and armed policemen stood guard. A group of tourists had gathered next to the memorial which marked where the Ghetto's inhabitants had been taken away by the Nazis. I found myself growing angry, then sad, at my own realisation that, in this haunting, humbling enclave of a great European city, its latter day inhabitants still required police protection. The story of persecution was not over. The hatred continues, and so the threat remains.

The Italian writer Primo Levi, himself Jewish, survived Auschwitz. He later wrote about this experience in the timeless, *If This is a Man*. Human fragility, and the fragility of human society, are themes found throughout his works. Levi was a living witness to the re-emergence of organised anti-semitism. To that vile, yet enduring, cause of crises and tragedy. In his collection of short stories, *The Periodic Table*, he wrote of the years before the Second World War, 'Our ignorance allowed us to live, as you are in the mountains, and your rope is frayed and about to break, but you don't know it and feel safe'.

It is a powerful metaphor, but not many of us like to think about the fraying rope. Nor do we like to think about the darker side of human history. But bad things happen with greater regularity than we might suppose, and crises are not exceptional. We might like to believe they are mere distortions on an upward curve marking human progress, but the Ghetto reminds us what the fall looks like when the rope snaps.

❄ ❄ ❄

During the COVID-19 induced lockdown, there was much talk about 'returning to normality'. This was understandable given the disruption people experienced, as well as the anxiety many felt. As a species, we like to feel we are safe, secure. When faced with changes to our everyday lives, we hope things will return to how they were. Familiarity, whether found in people, places or routine, is a source of psychological safety. A crisis not only threatens our *actual* security, it threatens our *feelings* of security.

The word *crisis* is, of course, of Greek origin. It originally meant a decision or turning point. It has come to mean a time of exceptional difficulty. The word may help us make sense of the world, but it can distort our understanding of events. Not only events in the present, but also things which happened in the past, or might happen in the future. The word crisis implies, and has certainly come to mean, that a phenomenon is temporary. That the unwanted thing will go away. We therefore fail to see that the causes endure, that they have, in some cases, accompanied us throughout human history.

There is a natural temptation to see the COVID-19 pandemic as an exceptional event. But if we adopt a long, historically informed view of disease, it can be seen as a modern example of the plagues and mass infections that have bedevilled human society. Some of William Shakespeare's plays could not be performed during his lifetime because theatres were closed to prevent the spread of disease. Philip Roth's novel, *Nemesis*, is set against the backdrop of an actual polio outbreak in 1940s America. Tuberculosis was killing large numbers of people well into the 1950s. Malaria kills many today. Advances in modern medicine may have sheltered us from mass outbreaks of disease, but they have also distorted our perception of the threats we have faced in the past, and as the pandemic demonstrates, may yet have to confront.

This speaks to some broader truths about human nature. About those stories we tell ourselves, about those innate traits which stop us seeing the dangers ahead. Throughout my career I have seen people overestimate their own abilities, while underestimating the probability that events could turn against them. I have a vivid memory of a senior executive in a successful company telling a large audience of his colleagues that they were living in a new golden age. As far as I could see, he had no evidential basis for the claim. When his colleagues asked him why he had made this claim, he had no answer. But only a few weeks later he was back on his feet, in front of an even larger audience, talking again about the mythical 'golden age', and poking fun at those who had questioned his rose-tinted view of the future.

What happened next was predictable: the business started to underperform, with lead rapidly replacing gold. And, as when Brian Cowen, the former Taoiseach, took a swipe at Morgan Kelly, a memory is created of the misjudgement, as it is of the manner in which it was made. It is often harder for a reputation to recover from the second of these two missteps.

Both examples illustrate the enduring relationship between hubris and nemesis. They also remind us what happens when we forget history, and when we exempt our predictions from the cycles which seem to govern human activity. Economies expand and contract, stock markets rise and fall. We are collectively confident, then we are collectively fearful. This cycle repeats, if not with metronomic precision, then with sufficient regularity to be familiar. We use the word crisis to categorise periods within this ebb and flow, but the rhythm endures, if sometimes unobserved. As Rudge, a character in Alan Bennett's play *The History Boys*, puts it, 'history is one fucking thing after another'. He ought to have added that it is usually the same fucking thing, even if the 'thing' looks different.

But we can escape our hubristic habits. We do not have to pretend we can see the future. Nor do we have to make a virtue of optimism in a way which obscures our ability to think clearly about issues. As Matthew Syed has explained in his book *Black Box Thinking: The Surprising Truth About Success*, some industries and businesses deliberately use examples of failure to improve. The examples he cites are striking for a few reasons. They involve the sort of long-term thinking we find hard and thus avoid. They involve putting blame to one side in the pursuit of truth. And the examples stand out as they implicitly reject our standard model for thinking about crises as atypical occurrences.

And this is the point. If we believe crises are exceptional, a deviation from the norm, then we will behave accordingly. Like the optimistic 'golden age' executive, we will be lulled into a false sense of security. Not only does this stop us thinking clearly, it prevents us from taking corrective action. This tendency is sometimes called path dependence, the phenomenon whereby we believe events will continue to follow the same or a similar track indefinitely. If we believe we are living in a golden age, then we will behave as if we are living in a golden age, with all of the consequences that will inevitably follow.

The nuclear power industry is a good, if perhaps atypical, example of how risk can be managed differently. Generating nuclear power is awash with the potential for crisis, bordering on catastrophe. The glass-half-full rules of commerce cannot apply. The worst has to be assumed. The resulting reframing of the task is incredibly powerful. It makes something very hazardous – splitting atoms – safe.

Something similar is true of the airline industry. The inherently unsafe business of attaching explosive containers to a metal tube, filling it with hundreds of people, and defying gravity has been made safe. Because a safety-first culture emerged in the airline industry, there has been a long-term decline in fatalities in air travel. We think nothing of sealing ourselves within the metal container as it hurtles through the atmosphere, giant jet engines raging either side of us.

Had nuclear or airline executives approached either activity believing, without any evidence, that a new golden age of safety was around the corner, we would quite properly cease nuclear power generation and we would travel by boat.

Executives in these industries have had to follow experts when making business decisions which have life or death consequences. They have also operated within stable and restrictive regulatory frameworks. Is it a coincidence that our recent financial and public health crises have occurred in areas where political influence has been strongest, lobbying has been intense and short-term thinking prevalent? There would be a public scandal if it were discovered that politicians had bowed to pressure for lower standards in nuclear power generation or airline safety. But this is precisely what happened in financial services. The issues in public health are different, but there are powerful interests in the pharmaceutical industry, and political interference in health policy is pronounced, for some good reasons, but with some undesirable consequences.

Following the global financial crisis, regulatory standards were raised. The amount of capital banks must hold was increased. Restrictions were introduced to limit the range of things they could do, especially riskier trading activities. Regulators became more involved in how banks operated. Without these reforms, the banking systems of many countries would have been weaker going into the COVID-19 pandemic. (I discuss where the financial system may emerge from the latest crisis in the final chapter.) This was an example of where long-term thinking led to long-term solutions. Although lobbyists had started to chip away at these reforms in the US under the Trump administration, regulators were, for the most part, able to defend the post-crisis standards.

Until financial services regulation is approached in the same way as airline safety or nuclear security, there will always be a danger that standards will be lowered during the good times. In regulatory jargon, this is known as procyclicality. In simple terms, this describes our instinct to relax or tighten standards at the wrong point in the economic cycle. The further we get away from a crisis, and the more confident we feel about the future, the safer we feel to lower our guard. This is what happened between the 1980s and 2000s as successive governments chipped away at regulatory standards, while allowing financial institutions to take more risks and grow in scale. This not only made the global financial crisis more likely, it left the financial system poorly resourced to cope with the resulting shock.

If we were able to discard the term 'crisis', or at least reframe its usage, would it make a difference to how we organise ourselves to be more resilient? Or are we, by our very nature, inclined to underestimate the probability and impact of shocks? Are we irrevocably convinced of our resilience as a species? Are we swayed by a belief in our powers of recovery? Or does the problem lie in political systems which lean towards short-term solutions? There is no one simple answer. Our use of language obstructs our ability to think clearly about issues. Crisis management is but one example.

But what if we were to substitute the term 'resilience enhancement' for 'crisis management'? Might this give us a different, and possibly better, lens on the issues we need to address? For example, if a government were to conclude that COVID-19 was actually a mild pandemic, and plan on something more serious arriving in the future, it would doubtless identify many opportunities to enhance the resilience of its public health system. Equally, if the same government modelled a more severe economic downturn as a side-effect of this later pandemic, it might organise the economy and financial system differently. This would, of course, have a cost. But this cost might prove to be a fraction of the price in lives and lost output from a further, more serious pandemic. Or, for that matter, a resurgence of COVID-19.

Government exists to make these choices in a range of areas: public health, transport, defence, education and so on. But do politicians and officials really internalise the lessons of a crisis? Or does the impulse to move on diminish our appetite to do the work necessary to make a society and economy more resilient? History suggests it is the latter. We may like to believe that crises end. What actually happens is that while the acute, short-term pressures abate, the underlying faults often remain. The crisis continues. It is just unseen, in the background. When the system is placed under stress once again, the faults become all too apparent. The problem, of course, is that those who did not fix these faults are likely to have moved on.

Until we recast how we think about crises, until we overcome short-term planning horizons, and until we take the work of building resilience seriously, we are destined to have to rely on being adept at improvising our response when the worst happens. As long as the worst is manageable, we will get by. But we cannot assume it will be so. Nor is it wise to put our trust in a reaction rather than a plan. We can mend or replace the fraying rope. Otherwise we might find we fall a long way, and further than we think, when it breaks.

Some lessons for leaders in a crisis:

1. **Watch for the fraying rope**. When things are going well, there is often little incentive to consider the downsides. This temptation is even greater in the immediate aftermath of a crisis. Either because people are simply glad it is over, or they want to move on. Even if things are trending in the right direction, it is the leader's responsibility to consider what else could go wrong, how the rope might snap.

2. **Make a point of studying extreme scenarios**. Our tendency is to underestimate the likelihood of extreme or disruptive events. A contingency plan is, therefore, only going to be as good as the quality of the scenarios used to inform its design. It is the leader's responsibility to make sure this work happens so the plan is meaningful when it is required.

3. **Be clear what you mean by resilience**. The further we move away from a crisis, the lower our appetite to do the work necessary to improve resilience. This dilution occurs because of the phenomenon of time inconsistency, whereby our view of the appropriate priorities changes over time. This is an obvious problem for anyone trying to build greater resilience into the system as standards can slip. To fight against this tendency, the leader must set a bar below which standards cannot fall. Regulators and boards of directors must ensure these standards are maintained for the common good.

12.

Endgame

For all of Patrick Honohan's ability as a mimic of foreign accents, he could never quite master the polished French-infused English of Jean-Claude Trichet. He had Mario Draghi's American-inflected Italian more or less nailed. His impersonations of his Troika counterparts were plausible if not always commendable. But the Frenchman eluded him. So he was not especially convincing when he tried to reprise Trichet after putting down the phone to him. It had been an important call. It was the last one anyone in Dublin would have with the ECB Governor before the stress test result was announced.

'We believes ze numm ber should be 'igher,' Patrick intoned. Dropping the French accent, he said, 'They want €24 billion.'

This was not the number the stress test had produced. It was, in fact, some way above this figure. Yet this was hardly surprising as the ECB had made no secret of its desire for a figure large enough to dispel doubts about the solvency of the Irish banks. This meant a number which could only lead observers to conclude the banks had been deliberately over-capitalised. In the final report published on 31 March, this additional figure was euphemistically called the 'conservatism buffer'. Had it occurred to me at the time, I might have suggested an anagram for Trichet instead. Such was the power of the ECB's Governor that he could request an uplift of €5 billion in a telephone call lasting a matter of minutes.

Trichet's conservatism had a sound rationale. He wanted to close the Dublin chapter of the euro area crisis. This might help to stop the fires raging in Athens and Lisbon. It might extinguish the euro area crisis before it spread to other capitals. Looked at in this way, €5 billion was a small price to pay.

He made his call as we were about to publish the third estimate of losses within the banking system within twelve months. Few had found the first two convincing. In the ECB's opinion, this stress test could not be a prelude to another exercise. It was this test or it was nothing. It therefore made perfect sense to inject as much capital as possible. In simple terms, the ECB saw a correlation between the size of this injection and the probability of success, with success defined as the government's and banks' ability to fund themselves in private markets.

But what made sense to Frankfurt meant further cost to Dublin. No one in the Irish authorities took issue with the ECB's logic. But there was little appetite to worsen the State's financial situation. A consistent refrain among critics of the bailout process was that Ireland would pay too high a price for its compliance with the ECB's demands. This latest request from Trichet added to a growing bill. This included the non-recovery of losses which might otherwise have been shared with holders of Irish bank debt. It included the extra costs of Emergency Liquidity Assistance when cheaper funding was available. Given this track record, it was not unreasonable to ask, as some did, whether the ECB was right to behave in this way towards a sovereign nation.

It was also right to ask what the ECB might do when there was a further €24 billion in the banks. Frankfurt had always viewed bank capital as a way of paying for loan sales, with the proceeds used to repay the ECB. Was Trichet's request a back door way of making this happen? We were certainly on our guard given Frankfurt's track record.

Patrick was also concerned that the banks themselves might suddenly start to write off loans at a faster rate. This troubled him. He had already clashed with the management team at Anglo Irish for this very reason. Not only was he concerned that value could be destroyed when prices started to recover. But because the State funded these losses, they resulted in more pressure on its finances. If the other banks saw an opportunity to follow Anglo's example, Patrick worried they would do so, especially where a new management team was in place. In banking, there is a long history of new chief executives taking pain in the short term to make things look better in the longer term.

As noted earlier, the ECB had always wanted its money back. In 2011, it remained uncomfortable at the amount of lending it was doing. But the reasons for its discomfort had shifted. With the Troika's financial backstop almost agreed, it did not have to worry about being repaid. The fear of default had driven it to distraction during 2010, and prompted its aggressive demands of Dublin. In early 2011, it started to talk instead about moral hazard, a perennial central bank preoccupation. It worried that its continued lending to Irish banks set a precedent. It did not want the euro area's bankers to believe it would come to their rescue if they ran into difficulty. As depositors in Cypriot banks were soon to discover, this was not a theoretical discussion. The ECB was serious.

The IMF recognised the moral hazard argument, but it was more concerned with the practical issues which problem loans created for the banks. Experience taught the IMF that banks which hold on to non-performing loans make fewer new loans. They also knew that it takes time to sort out problem loans, and that this distracts management from running a bank. In the IMF's view, loan sales could address both issues. No one in the Irish authorities disputed these arguments. Nor were they against the ECB being repaid and the banks funding themselves normally. But we did worry about the costs involved. We also worried about the effects of deleveraging in a market where asset prices were already in decline.

Here, again, the issue was one of timing. Loan sales needed to happen. We thought we had a better understanding of what was good for the banks and the economy. The challenge we faced, however, was that deleveraging had been one of the government's early remedies. The Irish authorities had already tried the IMF's approach when NAMA was created in 2009. This was designed as the nation's 'bad bank'. It was to be a repository for non-performing loans, allowing the banking system to be cleaned up. It was a good idea, but it quickly became unaffordable. The number of loans eligible for Nama were too great, and their quality was too poor.

The waning enthusiasm among Irish officials for NAMA was matched by the banks' opposition to further transfers. Richie Boucher was particularly exercised about the double-hit to capital and value recovery which resulted from

NAMA transfers. At one meeting he described the process as being the 'sort of thing that happens in a banana republic'. So what had been started in good faith two years previously was, by early 2011, a problem.

As we debated these issues with the Troika, it asked what had changed in our thinking. The answer was the lived reality of NAMA. When it bought loans from the banks, it applied a discount. These discounts turned out to be far larger than anyone expected. This had put downward pressure on bank capital in the 2010 stress test, which hardly helped an already difficult situation. This had incensed the banks.

Privately we had some sympathy with them. Not that this was NAMA's fault. It had a near impossible job to do, and expectations of what it could achieve were unrealistic. The loans it purchased often had very poor documentation, making its task that much harder. The efforts of its Chief Executive, Brendan McDonagh, were admirable. But the experiment was not working. Not only was Ireland getting little credit for NAMA's work, it was a source of stress in the banking system. It had been established with good intentions. It was therefore no surprise when proposals tabled for a second bad bank, named, with little irony, 'NAMA 2', received little support.

There were reasons to establish a second bad bank. The Asset Quality Review was pinpointing those problematic loans which had not already moved to NAMA. This population included those loss-making tracker loans which originated in the ultra-competitive pre-crisis mortgage market. These were not bad assets as such, but they were a drag on profitability. The interest rate the banks received on these mortgages was lower than the cost of deposits. These were a particular problem for PTSB as they accounted for a meaningful proportion of its total loan book. We spent some time considering what could be done to reduce the impact of these mortgages. One option was to move these assets to a new bad bank. As these loans were a drag on future profitability, funding them in a separate vehicle would help the banks' margins.

Such a vehicle could also have served as a repository for credit union's problem assets. This idea was considered seriously when we had some hope of restructuring that sector. Credit unions had little appetite, and even less ability, to manage non-performing loans than the banks. Taking these problem assets away from credit unions would have done them a great service.

There was little appetite to deal with the tracker mortgages issue. There was even less to restructure the credit unions. But the main objection to NAMA 2 was its potential to accelerate deleveraging. The Department of Finance feared that even the mention of a second NAMA might tempt the ECB to write it into the Programme for Ireland. This concern was well-placed. The Troika never gave up on further deleveraging. There were frequent exchanges about what could and could not be done to slim the banks' balance sheets. The effects on the economy and public finances were debated. But these discussions became circular. Everyone could see the economy and banking system were stressed. The pace and scale of deleveraging would either increase or decrease these stresses. The Irish authorities had one view of what was acceptable. The Troika had a different view. These differences of opinion remained unbridged at the end of the programme. This was, in its own way, a small victory for Dublin.

But the discussions about deleveraging were frustrating as they obscured a more important issue. We knew that it was only a matter of time before the economy recovered and asset prices stopped falling. Selling loans into a falling market exacerbated downward pressures. It also crystallised losses. We believed the better answer was to focus on the value to be recovered from those loans which remained on banks' balance sheets. By early 2011, private investors were starting to purchase real estate assets. They saw the potential for upside. As did the banks. And the sooner the economy recovered, the sooner loan values would do the same. But we barely discussed this issue. We had become so focused on calculating loan losses that we risked overlooking one of the basic truths of economic cycles. There was value in the loan books, as the subsequent decade has demonstrated. What we will never know is whether more value could have been realised had we given this issue more attention. We had no choice but to quantify the downside, but we could have done more to preserve value. This was, without doubt, a missing element of the Financial Measures Programme.

If we had more consciously pursued a strategy to preserve and enhance value, we would also have had to do some other things differently. All of them would have relied on cooperation from the banks. All of them would have required a more hands-off treatment of the banks from politicians and officials. But this did not happen. Public ownership has been a mixed blessing for the banks and for the country. It may have protected the banks from insolvency. It may have allowed the State to replace discredited management teams. But the banks' pariah status meant it has remained politically attractive to attack them, and it has also provided a justification for officials to interfere. Ireland was not the only crisis country where this has happened. Banking was politicised in most countries. But it has remained politicised in Ireland in a way which has hardly helped the emergence of strong banks.

The better solution would have been to incentivise management teams to maximise value from loan books. This would have benefitted the State and helped the wider economy. But it was never going to happen. No politician was going to reward bankers. This is a shame as more value could have been secured for the taxpayer, and the nationalised banks might have left public ownership.

But all of this was in the future as we worked flat out to get the Financial Measures Programme across the line. An increasingly tired team of Central Bank employees and consultants worked around the clock. There was little chance to switch off, and our emotional energy was directed exclusively at the Financial Measures Programme. The commitment I witnessed was inspiring. But it was also draining, and by February 2011, fatigue was fast becoming a risk to the project itself.

Tiredness can do strange things to even the most level-headed individual. The core group of Michael Feeney, Dermot Monaghan, Shane O'Neill and Dwayne Price were on their third stress test. They had been working on the same problems, at the same banks, relentlessly. The Troika, although mostly supportive, had created a further pull on their time. We all needed to be mentally sharp as some big decisions were ahead of us. The biggest of them all was the calculation of the important final figure for loan losses. Michael, Dermot, Shane and Dwayne were key to this calculation. It was obvious that the pressure was getting to them in different ways. But they were not alone. Not everyone may have shown how they felt, but feelings were running high.

The process of finalising the capital requirements for the banks was the greatest source of tension. This figure would emerge from two sources: the stress test (PCAR) and the Asset Quality Review (AQR). It would determine whether the stress test was going to work, and whether the State could afford to make it work. If the figure was too low, it risked being unconvincing. If the figure was too high, it might be unaffordable.

Tom Garside, who led the BlackRock team, had the unenviable task of performing the AQR calculation. He had assembled a group of technical specialists to perform the exercise. Tom himself was highly qualified. But the question on the lips of Irish officials was not whether BlackRock could do the work, it was whether it might do the work too well. A methodologically robust, yet financially crippling, answer was the last thing the Irish authorities needed. This worried Patrick in particular, and he stayed closer to this element of the Financial Measures Programme than any other. Tom knew, of course, that he was under a spotlight. Various attempts were made to draw an answer from him, but he steadfastly refused to give one before he was ready. We politely reminded him that he was there to do a job for the Central Bank. He politely reminded us that he had multiple stakeholders, including the Troika and his own employer, BlackRock.

Not that we were automatically committed to the output of the AQR. While quantitative measures do drive bank capital requirements, there is a degree of subjectivity and discretion in the process. We had to decide the level of provisions. We also had to make some assumptions about when to recognise losses. We could not avoid working with the outputs of capital models, but someone had to apply a common sense filter to the inputs and outputs. For more homogeneous assets, such as mortgages, we had little choice about using quantitative measures to generate a capital figure. For other asset categories, such as commercial property, where it would have been wrong to make sweeping assumptions about value, there was scope for a more nuanced estimate of the required capital. We had learned from the first stress test how the high-level assumptions about NAMA losses had affected the final result. We had learned that such assumptions tended to emerge from a rushed process where only poor data was available. Could it be different this time? It was finely balanced. BlackRock had its own reasons to be conservative. It did not have much time. While neither augured well, it had much better data than in 2010. This at least created a possibility we could use more sophisticated inputs than those applied previously.

Tom Garside also knew that BlackRock's name would forever be associated with the stress test. This had the potential to be good news for Blackrock's reputation, as well as lucrative for Tom and his team. But there were also risks to Blackrock. If the market concluded that another Irish stress test had fallen short, BlackRock would be implicated. If it concluded the result was overcooked, which introduced different risks, the finger of suspicion might point at BlackRock. But once it agreed to do the work, BlackRock irrevocably lent its brand to the exercise.

The initial findings from the AQR were shared for quality control purposes. This gave everyone involved the opportunity to query BlackRock's work. It was also a chance for the different preoccupations of the different participants to be shared. The resulting discussions were tetchy and inconclusive. The banks, of course, had much to lose, including some credibility with the Central Bank, if BlackRock told a different story to their own. They protested that they did not have enough time to review BlackRock's findings. While there was some truth in their claims, they knew it could only ever be a rushed process given the schedule.

Resolving these arguments gave Michael Feeney much to do. He stood between the banks and BlackRock, doing his best to supervise the process. This had meant, from the start of the programme, attending meetings between Black-Rock and the banks. He provided his characteristically wry and thoughtful assessment of the exchanges. Not being an expert in quantitative models, he sat through the arguments between the highly qualified mathematicians, physicists and engineers who made up the BlackRock and bank teams. I think he found them baffling and amusing in equal measure. Common sense and experience say that loan losses are highly uncertain and subjective. Borrowers are human, and as the future cannot be known, things might be better or worse than a model assumed. Michael was able to bring this real world perspective to what, otherwise, might have been mathematically rigorous but highly speculative conversations.

By the end of February, most of the inputs to the final calculations and report were ready. Some of the Troika's more experienced members were genuinely surprised at the quality of work emerging from the project. But there was still a risk that something unknown could emerge from the banking system that would invalidate our findings. And for this very reason, the ECB made its final demand at the final hour.

Not that any of this was explained in the report published on the morning of 31 March. By the time Patrick finished his call with Trichet, we were ready to publish a lower aggregate figure of €19 billion. The project team had already populated the report template. The print shop in Temple Bar, which had agreed to stay open all night, was ready for the document. Fortunately, we had sufficient time to make these final revisions. The only question was what to call Trichet's top-up. After some discussion, we settled on 'conservatism buffers'. It was bland enough that no one seemed to notice. Which is what the ECB wanted. Which is what it had always wanted.

Lesson #12: When we fix one crisis we always create another.

In a dark joke set in a Nazi-run prisoner of war camp in the Second World War, an injured British airman is told he has gangrene in one of his limbs. He asks the doctor to remove the leg and return it to his family 'so they have something to remember me'. The Nazi medic happily consents to this request. As the gangrene develops in the other limbs, the airman makes the same request. Only when he is down to his last remaining limb does the doctor refuse. 'We think you are trying to escape,' he says to the captured airman.

Unlike the imagined German doctor, we are not very good at spotting the unintended consequences of our actions. We are least able to spot them when we are denied time to evaluate the knock-on effects of our decisions. In the feverish atmosphere of a crisis, not only is there little time to think, there is invariably pressure to do things. There is often also a matching expectation to be seen doing them. This inevitably creates an atmosphere in which there is little or no possibility of decisions being evaluated properly. Only later do we discover their true effects.

This is not necessarily a bad thing. A crisis might demand immediate responses, particularly during its escalation phase. In a fast-moving, uncertain situation, there may not be the luxury of time. A series of rapid-fire decisions might be entirely appropriate. This is exactly what happened during the global financial crisis, where governments moved quickly to take control of banks, merge them, or allow them to fail. This was often done based on very limited information. But as the alternative was greater uncertainty and disorder, it is hard to argue these were unreasonable decisions, even if they were made imperfectly, using imperfect information.

The Irish government's decision to guarantee the liabilities of the country's banks is a perfect example of where a high risk decision was taken in the heat of the moment. Some attacked the decision on principle when it was announced. Others added their criticism as the cost of the bailout mushroomed. But much of this criticism misses two important points. The intent of the guarantee was as much psychological as practical. Equally, none of the decision makers could have known that Ireland's EU partners would force it to honour the guarantee. Put differently, Dublin rolled the dice, only for the EU to change the rules of the game. Whose fault is that?

Much ink has been spilled on the causes and consequences of the guarantee. But most of the commentary has failed to consider what could have happened had it not been put in place. It is not wrong to evaluate the guarantee by looking at what happened after it was introduced. But this does not tell the whole story. It is sometimes forgotten that it took the euro area another three years to resolve its own crisis. It is unclear that it would have been ready in 2008 to come to Ireland's rescue. Who is to say that the guarantee, because it gave the euro area cavalry enough time to muster, did not prevent Ireland been ejected from the currency union?

As a general rule, we pay too much attention to the things which happen, and not enough to the things which do not. This habit limits our frame of reference. It forces us to look down a linear track, where events appear to happen in sequence. It leads us to see connections where none exist. It obscures the random and unpredictable nature of events, the sheer weight of contingency. And when it comes to making policy, it means we start with an incomplete picture of the problem we are trying to solve. It may even lead us towards the wrong problems.

A branch of history called counterfactual history has sought to address this imbalance by looking at the past in a different way. Historians do so by asking what could have happened under different scenarios, rather than describing what did happen. This not only provides fresh insights on familiar events, it leads to a better understanding of *why* events occurred at all, even if the question of 'why' can only ever be conjecture. Like Sherlock Holmes, who solved a case by asking why a dog did not bark during the night, historians who look at what did not happen reveal far more about the contingent, random nature of reality.

This approach also reveals much about the messy realities of human decision-making. Many of our actions are unintentional, and many of our intended actions have unintended consequences. When it comes to understanding crises, we need to study what did not happen, as well as what did, if we are to gain a meaningfully thick description of the causes and consequences.

When it comes to managing a crisis, asking 'yes, but what if?' is a safeguard. It forces people to look beyond what they think they know. It compels them to consider alternatives. And unless there is a person in the room calling out the limitations of a decision-making process, the wrong actions will be taken, and the wrong problems addressed, with resources diverted from genuine areas of need. It will also lead to the sort of unintended consequences we see in every crisis, and have seen once more during the pandemic.

❄   ❄   ❄

We are starting to understand how some of these omissions and unintended consequences have shaped the current crisis. The most obvious omission is the failure of governments, with the notable exception of some Asian countries, to plan adequately for a pandemic. The most striking example of an unintended consequence was the impact on care homes of government policies designed to protect hospitals. Not only was the social care sector denied the resources it requires to protect residents. It appears that infected patients were moved from hospitals to care homes, sometimes without having been tested, in order to preserve capacity in acute care facilities.

It will take some years before a comprehensive and reliable assessment emerges of how public health systems coped with the pandemic. When it does, it is likely show that those governments which planned more effectively were able to respond more convincingly. We have to hope that governments will decide that transparency, rather than secrecy and evasion, best serves the cause of future disease prevention. If they do, not only will we learn what happened, we will also learn what did not happen before the virus spread. This will be incredibly valuable as there are obviously a number of gaps in our defences which need to be closed.

It will also allow us to evaluate whether actions taken to mitigate the pandemic might themselves be a source of future problems. In other words, we have an opportunity to educate ourselves about unintended consequences. The unintended consequences of not having done things before the crisis, and the unintended consequences of actions taken in haste during its peak. We will learn things we can use to improve the resilience of our public health and economic systems. We will also learn things about crisis management.

If the focus is on improving resilience, as it ought to be, then we might be able to prepare ourselves more adequately for the next crisis. If the enquiry process becomes a point-scoring exercise, or governments rush into reforms to be seen to be doing things, we will be at risk of missing an opportunity to become more resilient. Matthew Syed has written persuasively about how we can learn from failure in *Black Box Thinking*. But if we are to think differently, the reviews of the pandemic need to be different. In most reviews of a crisis we limit ourselves to the questions, 'What went wrong?' and 'Who was at fault?' We need to ask, 'What can be better?'

Whether we do so following the COVID-19 outbreak will depend on how we approach the task of learning its lessons. This education process happened quickly after the global financial crisis. In Ireland, the Honohan Report was published in 2010. In the United Kingdom, the Turner Review, which became a benchmark for regulatory reform internationally, emerged in 2009. Both reports led to the quick adoption of measures to strengthen the financial system. Regulators knew that in the immediate aftermath of the crisis there was a window of opportunity. They also knew it would close, and so they acted quickly.

The temptation following COVID-19 will be for governments and legislatures to initiate judicial and quasi-judicial processes. Neither the Honohan nor Turner processes ran on legal tracks. Furthermore, the reports' authors were subject matter experts. Legal rather than subject matter experts run judicial and quasi-judicial processes. This is wrong-headed. We do not ask lawyers to improve flight safety. Nor do we ask them to run nuclear power plants. Yet we expect them to provide us with recommendations on how to prevent and manage crises. We hope their work will help us prevent future problems, without actually asking whether either the process, or the people in charge of it, will deliver this outcome. These processes also take too long. By the time a report is published and recommendations made, the world has moved on. The Irish parliament only concluded its lengthy deliberations in 2016, six years after the Honohan Report was published. It is not clear what this achieved given the time elapsed.

Judicial and quasi-judicial processes also tend to focus on what went wrong *before* a crisis. We need to know what we did *during* the pandemic which may cause us future problems. We need to know what we *did not do* or have *yet to do*. We will have to live with the direct effects of the pandemic for years to come. But we will also have to cope with the unintended consequences of the measures taken during the outbreak. Time spent trying to understand them will be time well spent. And, arguably, time much better spent than exploring, through a lengthy legal process, what happened when.

But for this work to be truly effective, we not only need to ask the right questions about what we know has happened already. We need to invest the work with a purpose, to make it about improving our crisis management capabilities. The Honohan Report emerged before the most acute phase of Ireland's crisis. The country's banks and its economy were well and truly infected by 2010, but the worst was still to come. However, because it contained a reforming blueprint, it led to changes that made it easier to manage the next phase of the crisis. This was crucial to Ireland's recovery.

In a way, this is the main point being made in this book. Since we are disposed to see a crisis in binary terms – we are either in a crisis or we are not – we fail to attend to those issues which are the cause of future problems. This leads us to relax our guard, and it stops us taking preventative actions. This invites future problems. As the boxer Mike Tyson said, 'Everyone has a plan until they are punched in the mouth.'

Any claims of victory over the pandemic will set us up for a punch in the mouth. We need, instead, to tell ourselves two things. The first is that the crisis has not ended. The second is that we need to be preparing for the next set of challenges, including those we created from our early response to the outbreak. If we fail to plan, we can plan to fail.

In 2010, a new government department emerged organically in Ireland: the Department for Crisis Management. It had no official status, no office, and no employees. In fact, it was an entirely ad hoc creation, and largely unaware of its own existence. But this unofficial, semi-fictional department, comprising officials from across the Irish State, was able to get on with the job of crisis management.

The current crisis will last for years, and it requires a similar, if not greater, effort. We can escape the worst effects of the crisis if we organise ourselves accordingly. But this needs to be a multi-year endeavour. The second, third and fourth round effects of the pandemic will take years to manifest themselves. Some are foreseeable, such as the immediate economic consequences of lost output. Some are foreseeable but highly uncertain, such as the increased likelihood of corporate and government defaults. And some are unforeseeable, such as the social and political changes which might follow the pandemic. The world spent the 2010s adjusting to the consequences of the global financial crisis. Given the magnitude of the pandemic, the 2020s and 2030s are likely to be even more eventful.

Some lessons for leaders in a crisis:

1. **Look hard for the unintended consequences**. If it is hard to see the direct effects of events, it is even harder to grasp the consequences of actions taken in response to them. You need someone on your team with an ability to think about the possible consequences of different options. This will not guarantee that you avoid mistakes which come back to haunt you or your successors, but it reduces the likelihood of this happening.

2. **Beware thinking you have 'broken the tape'.** Reform does not stop because it is no longer needed, it stops because people have decided they have done enough. Crisis management requires unceasing attention to those things not done or left undone. It's a leader's responsibility to maintain momentum in this work. To remind everyone they have not run the race.

3. **Push hard for the things which make a lasting difference.** A crisis always leads to recommendations designed to deal with its consequences or prevent a recurrence. The benefits of these recommendations will not be uniform. And there will always be a temptation to do the things which are easier. It's the leader's job to reach a view on the actions which really matter, and then push them across the line.

A Post-Pandemic World

The drama of a crisis fades, but the effects endure. Many of them are obvious. Lives are cut short. Jobs are lost. Economic output falls. Government debt increases. Lifestyles change. Societies are different in important, if sometimes imperceptible, ways. But certain effects of a crisis are less obvious. And some only show themselves later. It can take us years to understand what is different.

What might be different after the pandemic? There are no simple answers to this question. Nor is there a single, universal toolkit we can apply to understand the experience and how it might have altered the future. There is no right or wrong way of looking at this crisis (or any other crisis for that matter). But we do need to understand what has happened, as well as our response to events, as our future will depend on the actions we take in the coming years. Our survival may not be at stake, but the welfare of billions (including the unborn) does depend on how we address the effects of this crisis.

What happened? The coming struggle for the meaning of the pandemic.

We will assess the pandemic's effects consciously, and we will also do so unconsciously. The logical, thinking part of our brains will focus on the practical consequences, of which there will be many. The intuitive, feelings side will try to make sense of our emotional journey. But whatever stories we tell ourselves, human nature does not alter a great deal, and the pandemic will not have changed people's fundamental nature. Even after the most cataclysmic events, the world has looked similar. If it were otherwise, we would not keep lurching from crisis to crisis.

This will not prevent the significance of the pandemic being debated for years to come. It is in our nature to look for meaning in events. This is the origin of history ('historia') as a field of study, and it is through stories, our own and others', that we will remember the crisis. There will be official studies and investigations. Writers and artists will attempt to capture the 'spirit' of the pandemic in novels, plays, paintings, music and poetry. But the degree to which these outputs resonate will depend, more than we might care to admit, on our existing worldview. As will the significance we attach to the pandemic. Some people will have been changed forever. Some will not have changed at all. And many will want to think they have changed as a consequence of COVID-19's visitation. An altered reality need not be real for someone to ascribe meaning to it, nor indeed to believe it is reality. Perception matters, and this crisis will, if it does nothing else, alter perceptions.

The economic consequences, however, are going to be very real, especially so for those nations least able to cope with the effects of the virus. Lost economic output means there will, for some time to come, be less to go around. Which is going to create some challenges as there are going to be more demands on these diminished resources as people look for greater security. This tension will have to be resolved as we normally address competing priorities: through the political system. The key question is *how* this happens. Will it be a harmonious process which emerges from a broad consensus about what needs to be done? Or will it be a more confrontational, fissiparous affair, where the territory of shared opinions is too narrow, and the politics polarised? The meaning politicians seek to attach to the pandemic will, for better or worse, have a major bearing on how effectively our political systems address the pandemic's economic legacy.

A new world order? Or a more polarised polarisation?

History suggests that when economic and social realities change quickly, so political realities and priorities alter in response. But what history cannot do is tell us what is going to come next. Nor should we try to extrapolate from the past without being honest about our reasons for doing so. We must be realistic about the limitations of such a venture, as we should be mindful of those who have attempted to do so in the past and been proved wrong.

In 1992, after the fall of the Berlin Wall, the American political scientist, Francis Fukuyama, tried to look into the future. He made some bold predictions about the dominance of western liberal democracy. He called this moment the end of history. I was a teenager when the Berlin Wall came down in 1989. For me it was just another news event, and I struggled to comprehend its significance. My parents, however, were transfixed by what they saw as a transformational event, and they did grasp its importance.

They had grown up in a world the United States and Soviet Union dominated. And although they lived under the shadow of nuclear destruction, they also inhabited a more stable, predictable world. The world has been less stable, less predictable since 1989, contrary to Fukuyama's hypothesis. Soviet power collapsed quickly, and American hegemony has been challenged consistently ever since. By Saddam Hussein (in two wars in the Gulf), by terrorists (on American soil and overseas), by China, by its own financial institutions, by internal populist movements, and now not only by a virus, but also by its own problematic handling of its repercussions.

None of these events is a direct result of the changes which began in 1989. But neither are their effects unrelated to the disappearance of that bipolar world in which two power blocs dominated global affairs. The world worked differently after 1989. There were global consequences from waning Soviet power. And since 1989, the US has, largely on its own, had to respond to the resulting challenges. And its responses have, of course, shaped the world in which we live today.

Similarly its response to the COVID-19 pandemic will shape the world to come. But what will this response be? Will it become more isolationist? Will it pursue multilateral solutions to the public health and economic challenges we now face? Will it work with China? Or will it confront Beijing?

There is a great temptation to see these as some of the key questions. But are they? Will the pandemic actually make that much of a difference to how the world's great powers organise themselves? Has it changed their fundamental priorities? And even if things are different, is it possible for one or two nations to shape the world in a way we once believed? Or are we viewing these issues through a framework which is itself now redundant? The United States struggled to coordinate its own response to the pandemic. Even if it had the political will to tackle public health issues globally, is it going to have the authority and credibility to lead a response? This is not the US of the Marshall plan, the Berlin airlift or possibly even the Apollo missions.

But even if Truman, Eisenhower or Kennedy were in the White House, would they have judged the pandemic to be of such significance as to require concerted global leadership from the US? One rather sobering conclusion may be that the pandemic, at least so far, has not been bad enough to trigger the sort of global response we saw after 1945 and, to a lesser extent, following the global financial crisis in 2008. This has been an international crisis managed almost exclusively at a national level. There has been precious little international coordination. And neither of the world's two major powers, China and the US, have emerged with their reputations enhanced. Nor have they shown any great urge to cooperate.

So while lives have been lost, and the economic shock significant, the world was not brought to its knees as it was in 1945. What some have characterised as an existential crisis may not have been existential enough.

It would also be hard to argue that the pandemic changes anything fundamental in the dynamic between China and the US. A trade war was well underway before the COVID-19 outbreak. The security and intelligence tensions between the two countries were also long in the making. The fact that the virus originated in Wuhan gives the US a stick with which to beat China, but its appetite to administer a beating will be determined by other, pre-pandemic considerations.

Is there more hope of global leadership from Europe? The power structures certainly exist. And there are incentives for Europe to push for international solutions. But the European Union has not had a great crisis either. Brussels proved ineffectual in the early stages of the outbreak, and there was no EU-wide approach to crisis management. Individual countries largely followed their own scientific advice. A blame game started only weeks into the crisis, with heads of state attacking one another and Brussels, mirroring the war of words between President Trump and state governors in the US. The net result of these public arguments, in both the European Union and US, was to make it look like no one responsible was in charge. This is hardly a foundation for global leadership.

But will the European Union's rocky experience cause it lasting damage? Here we have to distinguish between the words of politicians and actions on the ground. The different approaches taken in different countries illustrate the real political and cultural differences which still exist among EU members. The fact that land borders were closed is not insignificant. It will doubtless be said this was an emergency measure, with only temporary consequences, but will free movement of people across open borders be socially and politically acceptable in the future? How will those member states who imposed very strict lockdowns look at their counterparts who adopted a more liberal stance? It is possible that less will change about how the EU operates as a political entity than we might think. But it does seem plausible that people will feel differently about the European project. And not only as a result of the political fragmentation which occurred during the crisis, but also because of what this fragmentation revealed. There are different traditions within the EU, and despite the desire of many to integrate further, citizens defaulted during the pandemic to those national ways of doing things with which they were familiar, and which doubtless gave them a sense of security.

But the answer to these and other questions depends, in large measure, on how long we have to live with COVID-19. If a reliable vaccine is found, and mass immunisation occurs quickly, these problems might simply fade in importance. If this is the case, we might look back on the pandemic as a short, sharp but not hugely significant event in human history. Conversely, if the disease lingers, and we find ourselves in and out of lockdowns, the social and political consequences might be more enduring. Certainly those already opposed to globalisation have a new argument which, on the face of it, makes itself.

Under either scenario, we will want to believe we have seen the worst. The temptation for politicians will be to claim victory over COVID-19, particularly if a vaccine emerges sooner rather than later. Public attention will, inevitably, move on to other subjects if this happens. There will be an understandable human impulse to put the virus behind us, even if some may find themselves feeling strangely nostalgic for the lockdown. And it may be that citizens conclude that the loss of life, economic hardship and disruption, while regrettable and inconvenient, were bearable. If this is so then we are unlikely to see the emergence of popular reform movements which, in their turn, lead to lasting social and political change.

Or perhaps the political clock will have been turned back. Perhaps, having seen the power of collective solutions to a common threat, societal expectations will have been reset. The tide may turn against that trend, prevalent since the 1980s, of greater economic and social freedom for individuals. It may turn, instead, towards greater risk sharing, an increased role for the State and more collectivist solutions. If this happens, we may see the emphasis in political discourse shift from individual rights to individual responsibilities, and a greater focus on the needs of society as a whole.

Will the cure be worse than the disease?

The economic consequences of the pandemic will have a greater bearing on our future than its public health effects. This is not to make a value judgement about the relative importance of either. It reflects the reality that the resulting economic shock will have impacted more people directly than the virus. The world economy, on a certain trajectory before the crisis, has taken a different course. It is likely we will be dealing with the economic legacy for years to come, and this may include further shocks.

It is tempting to draw a comparison between the effects of the global financial crisis and the pandemic. In truth, the consequences of that earlier crisis were still being felt when the outbreak got underway. Economic growth was sluggish for much of the 2010s. Government debt levels, which had ballooned as a result of bank bailouts, remained high. In some countries, households and companies were carrying historically high levels of debt. Interest rates were exceptionally low. The scars from the global financial crisis ached when governments moved to respond to COVID-19.

The pandemic caused more damage more quickly than the global financial crisis. But will these effects be more enduring? Or is the nature of the shock such that the drop will be steep but the recovery sharp? The fact we do not know how long the effects will endure mirrors the situation we faced in 2008. For many months at that time, we lived with incredible levels of uncertainty about the future of the financial system. At its peak, the uncertainty threatened to become existential for financial institutions and governments. Would the financial system survive? Would governments default? Would the euro survive? As governments stepped in, the uncertainty reduced, leaving us to face the consequences for economic output and public finances. As the 2010s wore on, the effects of the global financial crisis were gradually reduced, but not erased.

It is important to draw a distinction between short- and long-term consequences. In the near term, until a vaccine or cure is found for the COVID-19 virus, we will be living with some level of uncertainty. Testing and contact tracing has the capacity to reduce this uncertainty as we will know more about the risks of contagion. But until we no longer need to manage the risks of the virus, it will serve as a drag anchor, particularly for those sectors of the economy, such as tourism, which rely on human traffic. This will be difficult, but manageable.

Much harder to gauge are the longer-term effects of the downturn and continued economic uncertainty. And not just the uncertainty which will persist for as long as the virus remains a threat. It is the uncertainty which arises from being less sure about our economic future than we were before the pandemic. This is where uncertainty can feed on uncertainty.

There has been much talk of a 'new normal'. But we do not yet know what this means for the nature of economic activity. Nor can we see how the social and political reaction will influence economic growth. Crucially, we do not understand the second or third round effects of the economic slowdown. These may be mild, in which case confidence will rise steadily. If there are a series of shocks, confidence may take longer to recover, and we could experience greater volatility in financial markets. The world was hard to read in 2008. It is much harder to reach today, not least because COVID-19 has touched every country in the world, and within each country, every single member of society.

It is worth emphasising the fundamental difference between this crisis and its recent predecessor. In 2008, the fall in confidence was sharp, but the bottom was found quickly. This meant the foundations for recovery were established not long after that crisis began. In the euro area, of course, the crisis lingered. But this was because the currency bloc delayed the exceptional measures other governments had taken many months before. Once an agreement was reached on burden sharing, confidence returned and the euro area economy resumed growing.

A better point of comparison may be the 1970s. That was a decade of multiple economic shocks. In 1973, the Organisation of Petroleum Exporting Countries (OPEC) announced an oil embargo, leading prices to rise by nearly 400 per cent. In the US, this led to rationing of gasoline and the introduction of a national maximum speed of 55 miles per hour. In the UK, the government introduced a three-day working week to conserve electricity. These were some of the observable effects. The broader economic consequences reverberated throughout the decade.

But although it is tempting to try to find comparisons from history, doing so is highly problematic. The world is a very different place today, and the world economy is different from that in the 1970s. It is true that economic activity and social freedoms were restricted by governments in the 1970s as they tried to deal with the effects of rising prices, but the source of contemporary restrictions is very different. Yet there may be some lessons for policymakers in how the consequences were managed (and mismanaged) forty years ago.

Beyond exceptional

In an early sequence in the film, *The Aeronauts*, two balloonists, played by Felicity Jones and Eddie Redmayne, try to gain height in a storm by jettisoning some of the contents of their basket. They are successful and continue their flight. But later in the film the balloon starts to lose altitude rapidly and they plunge towards earth. Only the improvisation of a parachute from the balloon slows the fall. But even then the danger is far from over. In fact, the real threat comes when the parachute, which had been drifting gracefully through the sky, strikes some trees, throwing Eddie Redmayne clear. Felicity Jones is then dragged across the ground, before the parachute comes to a halt.

The global financial crisis is the earlier storm sequence: dangerous, dramatic, yet manageable. In the global financial crisis, as in the film, the storm passed comparatively quickly. In economic terms, the pandemic is the film's closing sequence. In this crisis, as in the latter stages of the film, the fall has been further and faster. Like Jones and Redmayne, we will pass through further, and more dangerous, phases and, like them, we will need to improvise.

We can also observe that in the economy, as in the film, there is a relationship between the earlier and the later crisis. To keep the financial system and economy aloft in 2008, we threw a lot of things out of the balloon. We were right to do so. But like Jones and Redmayne, we entered the next crisis with fewer tools at our disposal, fewer options to keep the balloon from dropping. This left governments and central banks in 2020 operating at the limits of policy. There was little more they could do to maintain economic altitude and financial system integrity. Money was already inexpensive. It has been made cheaper still. Governments have borrowed even more. This only adds strain to already stretched public finances.

It is, of course, cheap for governments to borrow, so affordability is not an issue, at least for now. But a question which is going to haunt markets, possibly for years to come, is whether this debt might cease to be affordable. This is, of course, a perennial problem. At any given time, somewhere in the world, a country is wrestling with an oversized debt burden. But the debt dial has been turned again in response to the pandemic, and in a very significant manner.

The additional debt accumulated during the pandemic, and the further relaxation of monetary policy, will have an influence on markets for many years to come. The public finances of most countries have taken a battering. It is hard to believe that we will not witness an increase in market pressure on those governments hardest hit, with borrowing costs rising. Will this lead to sovereign defaults and debt re-structurings? Much will depend on how the global economy performs in the years ahead. If growth is sufficient to reduce unemployment and increase tax receipts, we are likely to live through a difficult but manageable economic future. If growth is weak, and if we experience further economic shocks, the likelihood of heightened economic instability will be that much higher. There is a risk that we might witness a series of self-reinforcing debt crises, where sovereign defaults create the sort of instability and uncertainty we have seen during previous debt crises.

We told ourselves that we escaped the global financial crisis because governments pursued exceptional policy measures. Governments and regulators did indeed do some novel things to bolster confidence in banks and the financial systems after 2008, such as direct capital injections, the effective nationalisation of many banks, and forced mergers. They then instructed central banks to start putting more money into the economy through asset purchases. These measures worked. Confidence was restored and, for the most part, normal economic activity resumed.

We are going to need to rethink our definition of 'exceptional' following the pandemic, not least because this crisis is very different to the global financial crisis. That started life in the financial sector, and ended in the real economy. This time we face a downturn in the real economy which has been far greater than we experienced in the wake of the global financial crisis. And these are the immediate economic effects we understand. Governments will be managing the longer-term effects for years to come. The exceptional policy response is going to become familiar.

An uncertain, volatile world economy

Sustained uncertainty has the potential to depress economic growth, as well as the performance of stock markets. It is also likely to promote volatility, itself a further source of instability in markets. These attributes can become self-reinforcing, exacerbating swings which, in turn, affect sentiment among consumers and investors. Governments can adopt policies to reduce uncertainty, such as supporting viable businesses. They can also intervene to deal with its consequences, such as stress in the financial system. But action at a national level is not going to be sufficient as we are facing a global challenge, and some countries will, as happened during the financial crisis, be overwhelmed.

There is a template from that crisis we can adopt to address this risk head on. The international response to the global financial crisis was coordinated through the G20. While far from being a perfect process, it sent a signal to markets that governments were going to coordinate their interventions. This was an important confidence boosting measure. It brought greater stability to the global economy, or at least reduced the likelihood of further instability. It also prevented a race to the bottom on regulatory standards. There was a consensus that banks needed to be made strong, and bank regulation had to be improved. International coordination following the pandemic will not change the economic realities the world faces. But it could allow us to manage the consequences which will arise from the interplay of debt and growth. It will not take long for markets to search for the weak links in the global economic chain.

How is the world going to deal with this challenge? We have the economic muscle and technical know-how to solve the indebtedness challenges of individual countries. We know that the pandemic will have a greater impact on those countries least able to afford the costs of care and treatment, and there is already a clear moral imperative to help them. To this we can add an economic imperative. The welfare of people in these countries will suffer where governments have to borrow more to address the consequences of the pandemic. The global economy will suffer if these countries grow less quickly or experience debt crises. How we manage these issues will have a major bearing on the long-term effects of the pandemic.

The financial sector as victim, not villain

The financial system largely mirrors what is happening in the real economy. It is by no means a perfect indicator. Financial markets can overreact in their estimates of economic performance, as they can undershoot. But we can get a reading from markets about what is happening in an economy, as we can glean from market sentiment how investors see the economic future. The health of individual financial institutions also reflects the underlying economic reality, with banks' loan books a key indicator of economic wellbeing. As we saw during the global financial crisis, not least in Ireland, when and economy suffers its banks suffer.

The good news is that banks entered this crisis far stronger than the last. Work done in the 2010s to strengthen the financial system had created a shock absorber. This protected the financial system in the first phase of the downturn.

It also protected the economy since banks were not only able to continue lending, they were able to make new loans. This prevented a repeat of the credit crunch we witnessed in 2008, when banks, unable or unwilling to lend, withdrew credit. That had an immediate impact on businesses and households, and it threatened to create a downward spiral which might have led to a depression.

Banks are, once again, going to be at the centre of events in the coming years. We need banks to perform the vital function of financing activity in the real economy. But only strong, well capitalised banks are going to be able to do so. And their appetite and ability to lend will depend on how economies perform in the coming years. If the economic consequences of the pandemic prove more benign than initially feared, the impact on banks will be commensurately lower. If the opposite proves to be true, the risks to banks will be that much greater. But under either scenario, it seems highly likely that banks will need to raise more capital. And this will be a good thing where it allows them to continue to support economic activity.

But how ready are the banks for the coming challenge? Loan books which might have looked healthy at the beginning of 2020 suddenly looked less so by the middle of the year. Economic growth might, as it did after 2008, repair some of the damage. However, as the stock of impaired and non-performing loans increases, there will be pressure on the banks to restructure facilities for borrowers. We will soon learn whether the banks have enough people qualified to manage this specialised, and sometimes difficult, activity. Modern banks have become giant credit distribution engines, relying on volume to generate profits. They are good at processing high volumes of plain vanilla mortgage applications. They are not so good at lending to small and medium-sized businesses. Nor are they good at working with these businesses when they run into difficulties. There is some risk, as in the earlier crisis, that viable businesses disappear because the banks simply lack the required lending capabilities.

If banks are unable to distribute money to where it is most needed, questions will rightly be asked about their conduct and performance. During the global financial crisis, the question on most lips was why banks had made so many poor lending decisions in the preceding years. The question they may face in the coming years is why they failed to make enough lending decisions during a time of economic hardship. A repeated criticism of banks is that they lend too much money to the wrong people, and they do so at the wrong point in the economic cycle. When businesses and households have a genuine requirement for credit, so the critics argue, banks prove less forthcoming. This is neither wholly accurate nor wholly fair, but there is enough truth in the claim, or at least examples can always be dredged up, to make it a perennial public relations challenge for banks.

But it will not help our economic future if the banks once again become a political football. Not only will this distract them from those core activities essential to the proper functioning of an economy, they will have numerous other difficulties to manage in the coming years. This new set of challenges comes at a time when many banks had only just recovered from the global financial crisis, and after a decade of costly regulatory fines and increasing compliance costs. They now face another decade of low growth, even lower margins and rising loan defaults. We are therefore likely to see some banks come under significant pressure in the 2020s. We cannot know how this dynamic will play out, but we do know that the relationship between a heavily indebted government and a weakened banking system is always intractable, and usually problematic.

But there is a potential trap in focusing too heavily on banks. We have such a clear memory of the global financial crisis that our familiarity may distort our frame of reference. It is highly likely that the global banking system will be more fragile as a result of the pandemic. But this does not mean it will be fragile in the same way as it was before the financial crisis. The banking system of 2020 is very different to that of 2008. For a start, it is more resilient. And it did not enter the pandemic carrying outsize balance sheet risks. Consequently, while we can learn a number of things from the last crisis, we should be careful to focus as much on the potential differences as the possible similarities between now and then,

And, as already noted, a major difference is the health of the banking system. During the 2010s, bank regulators worked to make banks safer. In broad terms, this was achieved in three ways. By making them hold more capital so they could absorb losses in the event of an economic shock. By requiring banks to use more stable and predictable sources of funding. And by restricting the risks which banks could take in financial markets. The most famous example of this measure was the Volcker Rule in the US, which limited banks' ability to trade. These and other changes meant the global banking system was in good condition when the pandemic struck.

But although banks reduced their risk-taking activities, these risks did not go away. Companies and households still borrowed, and investors bought and sold equity. An increasing amount of this activity was funded through non-bank channels, which was one of the intended consequences of the post-crisis regulatory reforms. The unintended consequence was to shift risk to those parts of the financial system less well resourced than the banks to cope with any losses. As the economic consequences of the pandemic work their way through the system, we will come to see where these risks reside.

We will also come to understand whether the unwinding of these risks might become a new source of instability. But again we need to be careful not to look at this issue through the lens of the global financial crisis. Risks unwound very suddenly in 2008 as confidence in the real value of assets on banks' balance sheets fell sharply. But this experience said as much about the fragile nature of banks as it did the underlying risks. The dynamic is likely to be different this time. In other words, when businesses fail, projects are cancelled and mortgage repayments stall, the knock-on consequences might only manifest themselves over time rather than suddenly. This does not mean it will be a less serious crisis. It may just be one where the effects are drawn out, and the costs slow to materialise. It may, put differently, be more 1970s than 2010s.

More money, ever cheaper than before

Governments will hope that the continuation of ultra-loose monetary policies, combined with government-backed lending schemes, will offset the worst effects of the economic slowdown. They will also hope it stops some of the risks taken in the 2010s unwinding in the 2020s. But two questions need to be asked. How effective will these policies be? And what effects could they have over the medium to long term?

We have just emerged from a decade of cheap money. This policy put a floor under the economy following the global financial crisis. It then supported the recovery in stock markets. Such was the performance of the major indices in the 2010s that we could be forgiven for thinking that we had lived through a new gilded age. And this is the point: did the deluge of cheap money distort our understanding of the underlying economic realities? Economic growth in most major economies was modest until late in the decade, and productivity barely improved. The policy of cheap money worked to bolster confidence, but low interest rates were always a sign of vulnerability rather than strength. The cheap money Band-Aid covered the scars from 2008, but the scars still ached.

The policy also meant there was less scope for further easing in 2020. Does this mean that the latest round of rate cuts and monetary expansion is going to have a more limited effect? The truth is that there is no alternative since any measure which protects the economy, preserves jobs and supports government finances is both desirable and necessary. But the harsh truth is that monetary policy will not, because it cannot, have the same effects in the 2020s as it did in the 2010s. The law of diminishing returns also applies to the price of money.

But has this point sunk in? Or, because we suspect it to be true, do we prefer to avoid confronting the issue? There is a somewhat worrying tendency to see monetary policy as a panacea. It is not hard to see why as it appears to have no negative consequences. It is also attractive as it enables governments to make less severe adjustments to public expenditure and taxation. But it is a mistake to believe that monetary policy can substitute for fiscal policy indefinitely. As it is a mistake to conclude that constant monetary easing can occur without negative results. History not only suggests there will be unintended consequences from a well-intentioned monetary expansion, it pinpoints a very definite consequence: governments find it very difficult to back away from this policy.

Although monetary policy can paper over the cracks in an economy, only sustained growth can fill them. Monetary policy has now been used expansively twice in response to two unusually severe economic shocks. This has so far been achieved without causing inflation. And it seems far-fetched, given the extended run of low inflation globally, and now given the economic chill of the pandemic, to believe that inflation might become a problem. But this may be the point: the absence of inflation is telling us something about the nature of the global economy which might be troubling. And it might be something we have known for a very long time. It might suggest, as the former governor of the Bank of England, Mervyn King, wrote in his book, *The End of Alchemy*, that global imbalances, and specifically the savings glut in China, have distorted monetary policy in the west. These imbalances were behind the global financial crisis. They have not caused the present economic shock, but they have certainly complicated the policy response.

Clearly no one knows for certain what is going to happen, nor how things will play out in the next decade. But two things need to be said. The first is that we have, once again, borrowed from the future to pay for today's problems. The second is that we have taken ourselves even closer to the limits of monetary policy. It is not clear that this renders the policy ineffective, but neither can we say for certain that it is going to be effective. The economists John Maynard Keynes and John Hicks described a situation in which conventional monetary policies, in Hicks's words, 'become impotent'. They called this the liquidity trap. There is no way of saying whether we have a foot inside its jaws, but it is an issue which policymakers need to address seriously, not least because we are running out of firepower to deal with a further economic shock.

Caring for ageing populations

Whether we pay the economic costs of the pandemic over time, or whether it will land on us suddenly and unexpectedly in another crisis, is to be seen. The seeds of the next crisis have almost certainly been planted in the response to the COVID-19 outbreak. But this does not mean we have to reap a bitter harvest. We have a choice. We can earn our way back to economic and financial health. We can make ourselves more resilient. We can, as Ireland did after 2011, recover from a crisis which, in its darker moments, felt like it might not end.

A major component of Ireland's exit strategy was austerity. Public expenditure was cut heavily in order to restore government finances. This was never politically popular, but it was socially tolerable. This equation feels very different after the pandemic. Not only has the virus killed some of the most vulnerable in our society, it has exposed major shortcomings in how we care for them. It is impossible to see how any government could cut public health and social care provision; indeed, it is very hard to see how they could get away without increasing provision in these areas.

This is not a new issue: we have been talking about the consequences of an ageing society for years. Governments have tried to deal with the problem by raising the age at which people can retire. Companies have done something similar by replacing defined benefit pensions with defined contribution schemes. And although it is well understood that an ageing population means a growing demand on public health and social care resources, we have not really addressed how treatment and care should be funded.

We have never had to face these issues before. There is no society in history where so many people have lived for so long. We rightly celebrate increased life expectancy, but there is a cost to caring for people towards the ends of their lives. The pandemic has been a stark reminder of the already significant demands on very limited resources. Demands which it is reasonable to expect are only going to increase.

But if there is a cost to providing proper care, there is also a cost to the economic inactivity which results from unemployment. I think it will take us a while to internalise this double lesson of the pandemic: we have more people who need better care and support, but fewer people working and therefore paying taxes to support them. Or at least we will have in the near term. This will put immense strain on public finances.

It will also, if for less obvious reasons, put a strain on our political systems. Before COVID-19, governments were already having to balance the needs of those in work with those of retirement age, whether or not they were in need of health or social care. Should those at work pay more taxes to support the elderly? Should older age benefits be reduced? Should people have to sell their homes to fund social care? The pandemic has sharpened the many existing questions about intergenerational equity.

In simple terms, these questions boil down to a single choice: how a nation's resources are shared between its citizens. Since there is now less to go around, while the demands on the State are greater, this leaves governments with some big decisions to make in the coming years. We need to grow the resources available to be shared out. But we can only do so if there are sufficient people in the working age population. Equally, public finances, damaged by the pandemic, need to be repaired.

Intergenerational tensions were simmering before the pandemic. It may be that these fade as a result of the stories we have heard, and images we have seen, during the pandemic. Perhaps our experience of intergenerational solidarity will endure. Or maybe it is going to be a fleeting experience when the new economic reality sinks in. When taxes rise, incomes fall or remain stagnant, and jobs are harder to find, those of working age will want to believe they are not paying more than their fair share.

Governments across the developed world were already facing these questions. They are now more acute, and more immediate. The good news is they are manageable, certainly for the wealthy, high income countries of the developed world. But tough decisions will still need to be made. There will, inevitably, be an enormous temptation for politicians to duck them. To hope strong economic growth will take care of difficult decisions. To borrow more today, and push the problem into the future. To kick the can down the road. This will not only delay the inevitable reckoning, it will risk a polarisation of society and politics. And as we are rediscovering, polarised societies and political systems do not achieve a great deal, and they are certainly more prone to crises, and quite possibly less resilient when they do strike.

Navigating the economics of the 'new normal'

We need to accept it is going to take some time to recover, and therefore we are in for the long haul. This is one of the biggest single lessons of the global financial crisis: the consequences of a major crisis endure. They endure in observable ways such as unemployment, home repossessions or business failures. The effects are also felt in things we tend not to think about. The roads, schools or hospitals which are not built because governments lack the resources. The mental health consequences of long-term joblessness. The businesses which are not created because people are fearful of the risks.

Ireland has much to teach the world about surviving a crisis. But it has even more to say about what can then be done to recover and rebuild. This has been called, in a different context, 'winning the peace'. It is the laborious work of putting things back together after they have been wrenched apart. It is the unglamorous process of making sure things work, not only when they are going well, but especially when they are not. It is, in other words, precisely that work which Ireland has been doing for over a decade.

Ireland, for the most part, won the peace. The exercise which concluded in March 2011 has stood the test of time. It finally broke the toxic link between the Irish State and Irish banks, allowing Ireland to emerge from the crisis and the rebuilding work to begin. The economy grew, debts started to be repaid, the banks recovered, if slowly and unevenly, and the Central Bank emerged as a strong, independent institution. The pattern of migration changed, with more people coming to Ireland and fewer leaving. The country thus entered the pandemic in a strong position. It not only coped well, it did better than many European countries.

Ireland is a small country, but it had to face a financial collapse as large as any in history. Its experience before, during and since the global financial crisis offers lessons as the world deals with the COVID-19 pandemic. As in the global financial crisis, governments were overwhelmed, practically and, to a degree, intellectually and emotionally. As in the earlier crisis, politicians and officials had to make imperfect decisions imperfectly. They had to sound authoritative when, in truth, very little was certain. It was a messy, uneven experience, but it created the conditions necessary for the country to recover.

In fact, far more was achieved. Ireland's crisis was largely of its own making. The economic and political rot had penetrated the foundations long before the banks started to show the effects. Irish people not only had the resilience to endure the consequences of the crisis, they had the gumption to tear out and replace the foundations. This involved some tough choices, as well as many years of sacrifice. It is true that the Troika accelerated the reform process. But it is also true that most of the work was done by Irish politicians and officials.

Had it been otherwise, the reforms may only have ever been skin deep, and they would not have endured in the many ways which are evident today.

Our only way out of the economic realities of the pandemic will be to address them in the same determined manner. We need economic growth to restore employment, repair public finances, and pay for health and social care provision. At an intuitive, emotional level, people understand that difficult choices are going to have to be made. They also understand there are no silver bullet solutions. But this does not mean there will be no public appetite for politicians who promise to limit the pain or make it go away.

Or, for that matter, an appetite for politicians who suggest that someone else should bear this pain. We witnessed a rise of populist politicians after the global financial crisis. These parties have consistently polled well in elections globally. Although some of them would object fiercely to the suggestion that they are the spiritual descendants of previous populist movements, much of what they say, and how they say it, is eerily familiar. The echoes of 1930s Europe are impossible to ignore.

The triggers for extremism, in both the 1930s and 2010s, were economic disruption, and a profound (and closely related) loss of confidence in established political leaders. We are not immune to a further rise in populist politics and politicians. And we would be deeply unwise to conclude that such parties will only ever have limited appeal. But if the pandemic has demonstrated anything, it is that simple solutions do not work for complex problems. Populist politicians may have some good questions, but they rarely have the answers.

Of all the strains of populism, the most dangerous, especially at this point in history, is nationalism. A global disease has, paradoxically, triggered a local, insular response. Nationalistic rhetoric has only intensified divisions, and done nothing to foster cooperation. There has to be a very real danger that global trade, and therefore global economic activity, will be casualties of the pandemic. No economic crisis in history has been made better by limiting global trade. International cooperation is required to ensure that trade, the engine of economic growth, can run at the required speed.

It will not take long before we know whether the prevailing global economic model – market economies trading freely with one another – will prevail. We need it to do so. It dragged us out of the depression of the 1930s. It fostered peace and prosperity after the Second World War. It has lifted millions out of poverty in the developing world. And it was, until 2020, enabling us to recover from one of the worst financial crises in history.

The choices we now make about our world

And this model can enable us to deal with another crisis which, although it may seem less urgent after COVID-19, nonetheless remains a threat to humanity: the health of our planet.

The natural environment has been a big beneficiary of the pandemic. Climate change activists will rightly point to these benefits, as well as to how they were achieved.

But the experience of lockdown is double-edged. Opponents of stronger environmental protections, in particular curbs on CO_2, will point to the economic consequences of shutting down much of an economy. They will argue that lower output and higher unemployment would be the inevitable results of an environmental lockdown, and it won't be difficult for them to point to the evidence to support this claim. They will also argue that an urgent return to business as usual is necessary to recover from the economic damage of the pandemic. We have to hope the debate will not become polarised in this way. The climate needs our attention.

Political leadership will be needed to unblock the climate change debate. As it will be needed in those areas where vulnerabilities have been exposed, or ways of doing things no longer looks sensible or sustainable.

The pandemic has shed light on the workings of those just-in-time production and delivery systems which typically run close to capacity. We rely on them to feed us, and when things go wrong, to care for us. Governments, officials and regulators will want to increase the resilience of these systems, while decreasing the points of failure. This could lead to far-reaching changes in supply chains, particularly if there is an impetus towards greater self-sufficiency in key areas, such as food production or the manufacture of medical equipment and vaccines.

There is also going to have to be a debate about how we work. Not in the sense of whether we work at home or at an office, but whether the flexibility of modern labour contracts is itself a vulnerability, not only to employees but to society as a whole. This is a practical issue, and it is also an ethical one.

We have seen that governments' ability to respond to the threat of unemployment was complicated by labour market complexity. There can be no question that flexibility has led to many benefits for workers and the economy. But governments found it much easier to support those in traditional employed roles than those on flexible contracts or who were self-employed. An interesting area for future study will be how labour markets in different countries fared during the pandemic. In the same way that a company's labour contracts have a bearing on its resilience, so the nature of labour contracts in an economy have a bearing on its resilience.

This may end up being part of a much larger debate about how we look after people in society, especially the unemployed or those on the least secure labour contracts. We know that work gives people much more than just an income. It is a source of self-worth, it provides status within society, and it can be an expression of purpose. But while the State cannot guarantee employment, the response of governments during the pandemic will have altered expectations of the role of the State. The unintended consequence of introducing an exceptional scheme to support individuals and businesses is that it ceases to be exceptional when up and running. It is not going to be impossible for governments to unwind these policies, but it has expanded popular understanding of the art of the possible. This could have any number of consequences, including a demand for some form of minimum income, whereby each citizen receives, in effect, a stipend. It is, more or less, what many governments have been doing in response to the pandemic-induced downturn.

But it may not be short-term government measures which increase the demand for greater social protections, including a scheme such as the Universal Basic Income (UBI). It could be the longer-term consequences of another period in which the value of riskier assets, such as property or equity, grow at a faster rate than the underlying economy. This will, again, be due to the fact that monetary policy has set the rate of return on risk-free assets, principally government debt, at zero, making it more attractive to hold riskier assets. And the effect will be the same as in the 2010s: to widen the gap between those who possess such assets and those who do not. In other words, inequality will increase unless governments adjust incomes for lower earners or taxes for higher earners.

Governments may not limit themselves to taxes on earnings. There could be increased pressure to raise existing levies on capital gains, as there may be to introduce new taxes on wealth. This will be tempting for governments who wish to reduce public debt. It will be attractive for politicians concerned with levels of inequality. And unless real incomes for lower earners rise at a faster rate than they have in recent decades, it is easy to see pressure build for the increased taxation of those who earn more and hold more assets. At the same time, the case to boost the incomes of lower earners through UBI or similar schemes might attract more support. Something will certainly have to give as the cumulative claims on the public purse will, as they did after 2008, only move in one direction: upwards. As will the levels of inequality unless something fundamental changes in the nature of the global economy.

But what changes might occur through societal mechanisms?

There has been much discussion of the short-term economic effects of not being able to work, travel, socialise and follow established patterns of consumption. It will take years before we understand the longer-term consequences. There are certainly many things we took for granted before the pandemic which, in hindsight, now look strange or unnecessary. Moving people around in metal boxes, or to congregate in buildings where elaborate cooling systems circulate germs, seems an odd way to organise society. Technology has demonstrated there are alternative solutions. But humans are social beings, and it is unlikely that people will have lost the desire for contact in a communal workspace. The issue, therefore, is not how we replace offices, but how we adapt them.

And what of our day-to-day habits, those behaviours and beliefs which make up most of our lived experience? Will we live differently after the pandemic?

History demonstrates that humans have an incredible capacity to rebound. Romans returned to farm the slopes beneath Vesuvius after its fatal eruption in AD 79. Life in Europe continued after the Black Death swept across that continent in the mid-fourteenth century. People still live and work on the same streets in London which the bubonic plague and Great Fire ravaged in successive years in the mid-seventeenth century. Locals and tourists still visit the beaches in Asia where the Tsunami of 2004 swept everything away so brutally. Life will go on, and it will, if history is any guide, be very familiar.

But this is not to say we will look at the world in the same way. My grandparents were born at the start of the twentieth century. They lived through two global conflicts and a Great Depression. They were in their thirties when two cities in Japan were destroyed by atomic bombs. They lived the second half of their lives in the shadow of a nuclear threat.

Three of them survived into the early 1980s. I knew them well enough to understand that they looked at the world differently from my parents. They were of that generation which made the world a better place. A generation which found ways to prevent and treat diseases which killed millions every year. A generation which did not fight a third world war. A generation which, if you like, found a way to deal with crises which were far more threatening to humanity than those we have experienced in the past two decades.

All crises lead to change. We will only understand what the pandemic changed when we look back in the future. But we are not bound to accept all of its consequences. Nor should we accept that we can do nothing about those crises which will, directly or indirectly, follow the pandemic. There are lessons to be learned from previous crises. There are rules of crisis management we can follow to soften the blow when they strike. But most of all there is always the freedom to ask how we would want the world to be different. How we might address those causes of crises which never go away, even if they fall out of view. How we might, as it were, look at crises differently so that we are more likely to prevent them, and when they occur be better prepared.

The Austrian psychiatrist, Viktor Frankl, spent his life trying to help people look at the world and their own lives differently. He survived the Holocaust, but his wife did not. He describes his own experience of coming to terms with its effects in his seminal book, *Man's Search for Meaning*. Frankl's message is that when we live our lives with purpose, we can overcome any challenge, setback or crisis. As he put it, 'In our response lies our growth and freedom'. That is always an option: to choose. And it presents us with a great opportunity today as we come to terms with our post-pandemic future.

Bibliography

Cardiff, Kevin (2016). *Recap: Inside Ireland's Financial Crisis.* Dublin: The Liffey Press.

Carswell, Simon (2011). *Anglo Republic: Inside the Bank that Broke Ireland.* Dublin: Penguin Ireland.

Central Bank of Ireland (2011). 'The Financial Measures Programme Report', Dublin: Central Bank of Ireland. www.centralbank.ie/docs/default-source/publications/financial-measures-programme/the-financial-measures-programme-report.pdf?sfvrsn=2.

Cohen, Leonard (1992). 'Anthem', from the album, *The Future.* Columbia Records.

Daly, Gavin and Kehoe, Ian (2014). *Citizen Quinn.* Dublin: Penguin Ireland.

Darling, Alistair (2011). *Back from the Brink: 1000 Days at Number 11.* London: Atlantic Books.

Donovan, Donal (2016). 'The IMF's role in Ireland', Washington DC: IMF Independent Evaluation Office. BP/16-02/04.

Fernández-Aráoz, Claudio; Roscoe, Andrew and Aramaki, Kentaro (2018). 'From Curious to Competent', *Harvard Business Review.*

Financial Services Authority (2009). 'The Turner Review: A Regulatory Response to the Global Banking Crisis', London. www.news. bbc.co.uk/1/shared/bsp/hi/pdfs/18_03_09_turner_review.pdf.

Frankl, Victor (2004). *Man's Search for Meaning*. London: Rider.

Geertz, Clifford (2000). *The Interpretation of Cultures*. New York: Basic Books.

Geithner, Timothy F. (2014). *Stress Test: Reflections on Financial Crises*. New York: Crown.

Hammond, John S.; Keeney, Ralph L. and Raiffa, Howard (1998). 'The Hidden Traps in Decision Making', *Harvard Business Review*.

Honohan, Patrick (2010). 'The Irish Banking Crisis: Regulatory and Financial Stability Policy 2003-8'. A report to the Minister of Finance by the Governor of the Central Bank. Dublin 2010. www. bankinginquiry.gov.ie/Preliminary_Reports.aspx.

Honohan, Patrick (2019). *Currency, Credit and Crisis: Central Banking in Ireland and Europe*. Cambridge: Cambridge University Press.

International Monetary Fund (IMF) (2015). 'Ireland: Lessons from its Recovery from the Bank-Sovereign Loop', Washington DC: IMF. www.imf.org/external/pubs/ft/dp/2015/eur1501.pdf.

Kahneman, Daniel and Tversky, Amos (1982). 'Judgement Under Uncertainty', in *Judgment Under Uncertainty: Heuristics and Biases*. Cambridge: Cambridge University Press.

Kahneman, Daniel (2012). *Thinking, Fast and Slow*. London: Penguin.

King, Mervyn (2016). *The End of Alchemy: Money, Banking, and the Future of the Global Economy*. New York: W.W. Norton.

Kohlrieser, George (2006). *Hostage at the Table*. San Francisco: Jossey Bass.

Levi, Primo (2000). *The Periodic Table*. London: Penguin.

Lewis, Michael (2011) 'When Irish Eyes are Crying', *Vanity Fair*. https://www.vanityfair.com/news/2011/03/michael-lewis-ireland-201103.

McGilchrist, Iain (2019). *The Master and His Emissary: The Divided Brain and the Making of the Western World*. Yale: Yale University Press.

McMahon, Jonathan (September 2011). 'Restoring Confidence in the Irish Banking System', *The RMA Journal. The Journal of Enterprise Risk Management.*

Mody, Ashoka (2018). *EuroTragedy: A Drama in Nine Acts*. Oxford: Oxford University Press.

Nyberg, Peter (2011). *Misjudging Risk: Causes of the Systemic Banking Crisis in Ireland*. Dublin: Government Publications. www.bankingenquiry.gov.ie.

Rajan, Raghuram (2011). *Fault Lines*. Princeton, NJ: Princeton University Press.

Sutherland, Rory (2019). *Alchemy: The Surprising Power of Ideas That Don't Make Sense*. London: W.H. Allen.

Syed, Matthew (2015) *Black Box Thinking: The Surprising Truth About Success*. London: Penguin.

Tooze, Adam (2018). *Crashed: How a Decade of Financial Crises Changed the World*. London: Allen Lane.

Index

9/11 attack, 23, 48
Aeronauts, The, 226
AIG, 26
airline industry, 191–93
Alchemy: The Surprising Power of Ideas that Don't Make Sense, 43
Allfirst, 25
Allied Irish Banks (AIB), 25, 85, 134, 153, 183
anchoring, 183
Anglo Irish Bank, 36–7, 65, 85, 134, 138, 153, 181–82, 198
Ardern, Jacinda, 16
Asset Quality Review (AQR), 150–53, 200, 204

Back from the Brink, 89
Bailey, Andrew, 94
Bank of England, 48, 70, 72, 89, 94
Bank of Greece, 164
Bank of Ireland, 85, 93, 134, 153–54, 183
'Banking Supervision: Our New Approach', 54–5
Barclays Capital, 148, 154, 180
Barings Bank, 48
Battle of Jutland, 57
Bear Stearns, 26
Beausang, William, 90

Bennett, Alan, 190
Berlin Wall, 218
Bermuda Monetary Authority, 24
Big Short, The, 59
Black Box Thinking: The Surprising Truth about Success, 191, 211
BlackRock, 152–53, 204–06
Boston Consulting Group (BCG), 155
Boucher, Richie, 94, 153, 199
Brady, Patrick, 36
Brown, Gordon, 94
Buiter, Willem, 88
Burke, Mary, 54
Burton, Joan, 179–80
Butterfield Bank, 26–27

Canary Wharf Tower, 23
Cantor Fitzgerald, 24
Cardiff, Kevin, 90, 114, 127, 130–31, 143, 172, 184
Central Bank (Ireland), 10, 12–13, 21, 34–40, 50–67, 93, 111–12, 128, 142, 147, 182, 184, 186
Charter of the United Nations, 123
Chopra, Ajai, 125–26, 130
Citizen Quinn, 36

252

Index

climate crisis, 82, 243–44
Cohen, Leonard, 44
contracts for difference (CFDs), 36
counterfactual history, 209
COVID-19, *see* pandemic
Cowen, Brian, 190
credit unions, 185–86, 201
Crosby, James, 136

Daly, Gavin, 36
Darling, Alistair, 89
Davey, Ben, 154–55, 180
Davies, Howard, 22–24
Davis, Gareth, 175
Department of Finance, 37, 73, 90, 142, 144, 147, 168, 184
Department for Crisis Management, 214
deposit insurance scheme (UK), 93
Duffy, David, 154

EBS, 134, 183
Economic Adjustment Programme for Ireland, 134
Elderfield, Matthew, 22, 24, 27, 35, 53–4, 64, 67, 85, 91, 129, 143, 145–46, 148, 151
Emergency Liquidity Assistance (ELA), 72–4, 112, 197
End of Alchemy, The, 236
Enria, Andrea, 76
Equitable Life, 23
European Banking Authority (EBA), 64
European Central Bank (ECB), 52, 70–7, 108–17, 126–29, 131–33, 155, 171, 184, 196–99, 201, 206
European Commission (EC), 88, 127, 184
European Union, 221

EuroTragedy: A Drama in Nine Acts, 132

Federal Reserve (US), 70–1
Feeney, Michael, 56, 203, 206
Ferguson Alex, 118–19
Financial Conduct Authority (UK), 94
Financial Measures Programme, 134, 142, 146, 151, 158, 180–81, 184, 202–04
Financial Regulator (Ireland), 21, 22, 27, 36, 121
Financial Services Authority (UK), 22, 23, 170
Financial Services Commission (FSC) (Isle of Man), 85–8
Financial Times, 55, 88
Fine Gael, 181
Fink, Larry, 152
Fog of War, 135
Foot, Michael, 22–24, 48
Frankl, Viktor, 248
Free Solo, 173
Fukuyama, Francis, 218

G20, 5, 229
Garda Síochána, 165
Garside, Tom, 204–05
Geertz, Clifford, 29
George, Eddie, 48
Gilmore, Eamon, 180
Goodwin, Fred, 25, 136
Great Depression, 2, 27, 247
Greece, 40, 68, 70, 74, 109, 112, 115, 126

Hadfield, Chris, 18
Halifax Bank of Scotland, 136, 183
haruspex, 14
Harvard Business Review, 58, 135
Hicks, John, 237

'Hidden Traps in Decision Making', 135

History Boys, The, 190

Holmes, Sherlock, 209

Honnold, Alex, 173–74

Honohan, Patrick, 28, 35, 52–4, 64, 67, 114, 129–31, 143, 146–48, 152, 165–68, 172, 196–98, 207

Honohan Report, 212–13

Horan, Con, 21

Hostage at the Table, 81

Hussein, Saddam, 219

If This is a Man, 188

Independent Insurance, 23

International Financial Services Centre, 144

International Monetary Fund (IMF), 78, 116–17, 125–33, 199

Irish League of Credit Unions (ILCU), 185–86

Irish Life, 154

Irish Nationwide Building Society, 153, 182

Irish Republican Army (IRA), 23

Irish Stock Exchange, 21

Isle of Man, 84–8

Japan, 115

Jellicoe, John, 57

Johnson, Boris, 17

'Judgement Under Uncertainty', 18

Julius Caesar, 14

Kahneman, Daniel, 18, 183

KBC Bank, 183

Keating, Andrew, 153

Keegan, Kevin, 118–19

Kehoe, Ian, 36

Kelly, Morgan, 80, 111, 190

Kenny, Enda, 180

Keynes, John Maynard, 237

Kierkegaard, Søren, 49

King Lear, 79

King, Mervyn, 236

Kingman, John, 147

Kingsbury, Donald, 3

Kipling, Rudyard, 2

Kohlrieser, George, 81

Labour Party (Irish), 179–81

Leeson, Nick, 48

Lehman Brothers, 26

Lenihan, Brian, 38

Lenin, Vladimir, 78

Levi, Primo, 188

Lewis, Michael, 59, 121

Long Term Capital Management, 23

Ludwig, Eugene, 25

Macpherson, Nick, 90

Maher, Michael, 128

Manchester United, 117–19

Mandelson, Peter, 93

Marshall Plan, 123

Master and His Emissary, The, 100

Masuch, Klaus, 110, 132

McAleese, Mary, 119–20

McCarthy, Callum, 22

McCarthy, Colm, 121

McDonagh, Brendan, 200

McDowell, Andrew, 180–81

McGilchrist, Iain, 100

McNamara, Robert, 135, 140

Merkel, Angela, 16

Mody, Ashoka, 78, 131–33

Monaghan, Dermot, 56, 203

Moneyball, 59

Moran, John, 56, 180, 182

Morning Ireland, 129

Murphy, David, 55

NAMA 2 option, 181, 200–01
Nascimento, Afonso, 155
National Asset Management
  Agency (NAMA), 64–5, 67,
  151, 199–201, 205
National Traffic and Motor Vehi-
  cle Safety Act (US), 62
Neary, Patrick, 21, 27, 121
Nelson, Horatio, 57
Nemesis, 189
Newcastle United, 117–19
Noonan, Michael, 114, 180
Northern Rock, 26, 94, 98
nuclear power, 191–93

Obama, Barack, 165
Ó Caoláin, Caoimhghín, 10–12
O'Neill, Shane, 56, 64, 203
Organization of the Petroleum
  Exporting Countries (OPEC),
  225
Osborne, George, 89

pandemic
  ageing populations and,
    237–40
  changing world of work and,
    244–46
  compared to global financial
    crisis, 223–28
  economic consequences of,
    223
  financial sector and, 230–34
  leadership during, 122–24,
    139–40
  meaning of, 216–18
  monetary policies during,
    234–37
  uncertainty and, 15–20, 47–48,
    104
Periodic Table, The, 188
Permanent TSB (PTSB), 134,
  154, 183–84, 200

PIGS (Portugal, Ireland, Greece,
  Spain), 40
'pillar banks', 182–84
Plimsoll, Samuel, 62
polarisation, 218–23
populism, 242
Portugal, 40, 68, 70, 74, 109, 115,
  126
Post Office (UK), 93
Price, Dwayne, 56, 84, 87, 164,
  203
Project Greenfield, 170
Promontory Financial Group,
  25–26
Prudential Capital Assessment
  Review (PCAR), 150, 204
Prudential Regulatory Authority
  (UK), 94
public health systems, 8, 16,
  19,123, 139–40, 177, 192, 194,
  219–20, 238

Queen Elizabeth, 84, 119–20,
  165
Quinn Group, 37–39, 91, 138
Quinn Insurance, 10, 12–13,
  36–40, 90–2, 96
Quinn, Sean, 10, 12–14, 36–40

Railtrack, 23
Robinson, Mary, 119
Ross, Wilbur, 186
Roth, Philip, 189
Rothschild, 147
Royal Bank of Scotland (RBS),
  25–27, 72, 136

Sheldon, C. Hunter, 62
Single Market (European), 76,
  172
Sinn Féin, 10–11, 179
Sisyphus, 9
Socrates, 59

Special Resolution Scheme (UK), 94

Special Resolution Unit, 94–5

stress tests, 64–9, 142–58

Sunk Cost Trap, 135–36

Sutherland, Rory, 43

Syed, Matthew, 190, 211

Thatcher, Margaret, 120

'The Way through the Woods', 2

Thinking, Fast and Slow, 183

Trichet, Jean-Claude, 196–97, 207

Troika, 45, 117, 126–34, 142–45, 165, 168–70, 172, 181, 196, 201, 206

Trump, Donald, 17, 103

Turner Review, 212

Tversky, Amos, 18

Tyson, Mike, 213

Ulster Bank, 183

Universal Basic Income (UBI), 245–46

van de Velde, Jean, 40–42

Vanity Fair, 121

Varadkar, Leo, 180

Venice, 187–88

Vidal, Gore, 61

Wall Street Journal, 55

Watson, Thomas J., 59

Wodehouse, Richard, 138

Zehnder, Egon, 58